COOKING
with Love,
ITALIAN
STYLE

COOKING
with Love,
ITALIAN
STYLE

FRANCIS ANTHONY

HEARST BOOKS / NEW YORK

It is the policy of William Morrow and Company, Inc., and its imprints and affiliates, recognizing the improtance of preserving what has been written, to print the books we publish on acid-free paper, and we exert our best efforts to that end.

Library of Congress Cataloging-in-Publication Data

Anthony, Francis.
Cooking with love, Italian style / by Francis Anthony.
p.   cm.
Includes index.
ISBN 0-688-12754-1
1. Cookery, Italian.   I. Title.
TX723.A55   1994

641.5945—dc20

93-43045
CIP

Printed in the United States of America

7 8 9 10

BOOK DESIGN BY GIORGETTA BELL MCREE

This book is dedicated to the talented Italians
who guided me in my formative years:

Mom Theresa
Dad Andrew
Brother Andrew
Aunt Ida
Uncle Tony
Uncle Sal
Uncle John
Uncle Joe
and in memory of
Grandma Jenny
Grandpa Frank
and all my family and friends who keep me
cooking with love.

CONTENTS

INTRODUCTION

*T*here is nothing like the ritual of sitting down to an Italian table. The family is brought together in love of each other and in love of good food. Along with the *minestra* and stuffed beef, salad and espresso, we are nourished by the animated conversation. Dreams are dreamed, life decisions are discussed, sometimes even confessions are heard. An Italian meal is orchestrated to heal all wounds, to nourish both body and soul!

There is always a place for a guest to join the table. Even today I can call Mom at the last minute and say, "I'm coming to dinner," and a meal that started as just a simple dinner for Dad and her turns into a feast.

Sometimes it takes us ninety years to appreciate the gifts God has given us, but I can truly say that from the day I was old enough to hold a fork, never a dinnertime went by that I didn't give thanks for my family's Italian traditions. The diversity of tastes is anything but tomato sauce only.

Just-picked vegetables and fruits were especially important at our house. Since boyhood, Dad had worked in the two green groceries owned by my grandfather. In fact, Dad was given the assignment of taking the peddler's wagon pulled by a white horse and hawking his fresh produce through New York's streets. It was on his route that he met pretty young Theresa, the nursing school student who would become his wife.

The family grew strong on Mom's pastas and light sauces, the touches of garlic, the moderate use of olive oil, all of which have been proven excellent for body as well as soul. The fun shapes of spaghetti and other pasta and the easy-to-handle pizza slices made Italian the favorite food of even the youngest children and grandchildren in the family. And the generosity of the Italian cook assures that every appetite is sated.

In fact, when I prepare recipes on national television shows like *Live with Regis and Kathie Lee* or my own show seen in many local areas, the most often-requested recipes are Italian.

I get a kick out of people who take me aside and try to get me to reveal my favorite food. They figure that being in the business I secretly have developed a love for fancy recipes made with expensive, rare ingredients from other planets. Here's the answer. What do I like to cook? What do I like to serve my family and friends? What do I like to eat? Italian, Italian, and more Italian.

And it is Italian food that we all can share. Italian that considers today's nutritional needs. Italian that doesn't take all day to prepare. Italian that any family can afford. It's my mom's Italian, my dad's Italian. My aunt Josie's Italian, my uncle Tony's Italian. It's my kind of Italian—Italian *con amore!*

CHAPTER 1

&

Appetizers / Starters / Hors d'oeuvres
Antipasti

*E*very cuisine has its "little dishes," tastings to tease the palate for the main event that follows. In Italian cooking, they are the antipasti, diverse hot and cold samplings served before the pasta.

Often a family skips the antipasti and plunges right into the soup. They are missing an opportunity for relaxed family talk while the cook of the day puts the finishing touches on the main course. Antipasti also offer an opportunity for the adults of the family to savor a glass of wine while they nibble on a special piece of prosciutto or salami, roasted peppers, bruschetta, marinated olives, oysters and shrimp, ripe tomatoes, fresh herbs, and the nectar of the gods—olive oil. Why wait for guests to enjoy antipasti!

GRILLED BREAD
Bruschetta

In the summertime, my dad's abundant crop of vine-ripened tomatoes, along with his fresh basil, offers a great excuse to make this appetizer. It's perfect with cocktails while we're out back getting the barbecue going.

This salad also brings back memories of a 3½-hour lunch in Tuscany during which fabulous grilled treats kept appearing as if by magic.

8 slices Italian bread, about ½ inch thick
2 tablespoons extra-virgin olive oil
2 cloves garlic, crushed
Freshly ground black pepper to taste
Pinch dried thyme
Salt to taste (optional)
Fresh basil leaves
2 ripe tomatoes, chopped (about 1 cup)

Serves 4

Toast the bread on a grill (or under a broiler), turning so that both sides are toasted. In a small bowl, mix the oil, garlic, pepper, thyme, and salt. Brush this mixture on top of the toasted bread, add basil leaves and a mound of tomatoes, and you are ready to serve.

Pinzimonio

Since the name of this appetizer means "to pinch or grasp" in Italian, it is the counterpart of the French crudités—assorted raw vegetables. I recommend that fennel, often called Italian celery, be used when in season.

This Italian version is terrific with a number of condiments, including those mentioned below.

1 bunch scallions, trimmed
1 large bulb fennel or celery, cut into bite-size pieces
3 carrots, cut into wide ribbons
1 bunch small radishes, trimmed

DIPPING CONDIMENTS
Extra virgin olive oil
Balsamic vinegar
Mixture of freshly ground black pepper and salt

Artistically arrange the vegetables on a large platter, with bowls of the three dipping condiments clustered around.

OYSTERS AND SHRIMP
Ostriche e Gamberi

In the Lake Como region of Italy, I happened upon a neighborhood restaurant for lunch. The display of seafood dishes on the antipasti table was awesome. Using the freshest seafood, this is the closest I have been able to come to re-creating that feast. Of course, it tastes all the better with a breathtaking view of Lake Como!

2 cloves garlic
1 small onion, quartered
1 stalk celery, sliced
½ carrot, thinly sliced
¼ cup olive oil
1 pound medium shrimp, peeled and deveined
18 oysters, shucked and cleaned (you may substitute mussels)
1 teaspoon drained capers
Juice of 1 lemon
¼ cup chopped Italian parsley
Freshly ground black pepper to taste
Salt to taste (optional)

Serves 4 to 6

In a large skillet, sauté the garlic, onion, celery, and carrot in the olive oil. When the garlic is golden, remove and discard it. Add the shrimp and oysters and sauté for approximately 5 minutes, until the shrimp are pink. With a slotted spoon, remove the shellfish and vegetables and place in a bowl. Add the capers, lemon juice, parsley, pepper, and salt and toss together.

Let the dish marinate in the refrigerator for a few hours before serving.

Sweet Roasted Peppers with Sausage in Pita Bread

Pita con Peperoni e Salsiccie

1½ pounds sweet Italian sausages
3 7¼-ounce jars sweet roasted peppers
2 tablespoons unsalted butter
Pinch dried oregano
Pinch dried parsley
Freshly ground black pepper to taste
12 mini pita breads, cut in half

Yields approximately 24 hors d'oeuvres

In a saucepan, parboil the sausages for about 5 minutes. Allow them to cool and then finely chop by hand or in a food processor.

Drain the peppers and finely chop them by hand or in the food processor.

In a large skillet, melt the butter and add the chopped peppers. Stir in the chopped sausages, oregano, parsley, and ground pepper and sauté over medium heat for 12 to 15 minutes.

Serve in small pita bread pockets. Or grind finer and use as a spread on small rounds of French bread or on endive leaves.

Mozzarella in a Carriage
Mozzarella in Carrozza

This oddly named little treat is seen on many an Italian restaurant menu. I've lightened up the traditional version by using low-fat cheese and milk. Kids love the mozzarella cheese oozing out of the deep-fried bread. Makes a great party hors d'oeuvre for both young and old.

6 thick slices mozzarella cheese, low-fat or no fat
12 slices stale white bread, thinly sliced, crusts cut off
⅛ teaspoon dried thyme
⅛ teaspoon white pepper
2 egg whites plus 1 whole egg, beaten
½ cup 1% low-fat milk
½ cup bread crumbs
Oil for frying

Yields 12 pieces

Make 6 sandwiches with the mozzarella slices and bread, then cut each in half to make 12 triangles. Add thyme and pepper to the beaten eggs and mix thoroughly.

Triangles can be held together with wooden toothpicks.

Dip each sandwich in milk, then in egg and bread crumbs, and deep-fry.

Oven Method: Preheat the oven to 450°F. Lightly grease a cookie sheet.

Place prepared sandwiches on greased cookie sheet and bake until golden brown, 15 to 18 minutes.

STUFFED TUSCAN PEPPERS

Peperoncini Ripieni

These little green peppers are also called peperoncini. Pickled and jarred, they are mildly hot, and when combined with this stuffing, they make great cocktail nibbles.

1 9-ounce jar Tuscan peppers
2 anchovy fillets, drained, washed, and patted dry
2 ounces cream cheese or mascarpone
Pinch cayenne pepper

Yields approximately 18 hors d'oeuvres

Drain the peppers and make a lengthwise slit in each. In a bowl, mash the anchovies with the cream cheese and cayenne pepper. Using a pastry bag or a knife, fill each pepper.

ENDIVE WITH CHEESE

Indive con Formaggio

I like to serve these little bites with wine or cocktails. The silky cheese mixture is perfect with the crispness of the endive.

4 ounces mascarpone cheese
½ teaspoon Dijon mustard
¼ teaspoon Worcestershire sauce
Pinch white pepper
1 Belgian endive, washed and separated into leaves
1 tablespoon chopped Italian parsley

Yields 12 to 15 pieces

In a small bowl, mix the mascarpone cheese, mustard, Worcestershire sauce, and pepper. Spread mixture on endive leaves and sprinkle with chopped parsley. Arrange on a platter and serve.

GARLIC AND ANCHOVY BATH

Bagna Caôda

This old-time Italian dip is simplicity itself.

8 ounces (1 cup) unsalted butter
¾ cup extra-virgin olive oil
4 cloves garlic, finely chopped
6 anchovy fillets, rinsed
Freshly ground black pepper to taste

Yields enough to coat 4 to 5 dozen pieces of vegetables

Prepare fresh vegetables of your choice for dipping, such as celery sticks, cucumber and tomato wedges, cauliflower florets, zucchini slices, and pepper quarters.

In a medium skillet, heat the butter and olive oil, add the garlic, and gently sauté for a few minutes. Add the anchovies and stir until they dissolve. Add pepper. In the meantime, set a chafing dish over a low flame. Transfer garlic-anchovy mix from skillet to chafing dish. Maintain low heat.

When ready to serve, place chafing dish on the table. Guests should spear vegetables with long wooden skewers and immerse them in the hot dip for a few seconds.

MARINATED EGGPLANT
Melanzane Marinate

Serve a small amount of these marinated eggplants alongside traditional dried salami or pepperoni as a little savory starter.

2 medium, firm eggplants (about 2½ pounds total)
Salt to taste (optional)
3 cloves garlic, minced
1 tablespoon dried sage
Freshly ground black pepper to taste
Extra-virgin olive oil
½ cup balsamic vinegar

Serves 6 to 8

Cut eggplant (with peel on) lengthwise into ½-inch-thick slices. Sprinkle them with salt, place in a colander, and let stand in sink for about an hour to purge the eggplant of any bitter juices. Pat eggplant slices dry with paper towels.

Mix together the garlic, sage, and salt and pepper to taste.

Layer the eggplant on a serving dish brushed with olive oil. Cover each layer with a little of the garlic mixture and repeat until all of the eggplant is used.

Now pour the vinegar over all, cover, and let stand in the refrigerator for several hours, turning slices over once.

Serve at room temperature.

EGGPLANT RELISH

Caponata

This popular southern Italian dish is a versatile appetizer spread. I've even enjoyed it as a midnight snack spread on a few slices of Italian bread or crackers. The flavor improves with age, so when possible, make it the day before you plan to serve it.

2 cups diced celery
½ cup olive oil
1 large or 2 medium eggplants, peeled and diced (about 6 cups)
1 onion, chopped
2 tablespoons tomato paste
¾ cup water
⅓ cup red wine vinegar
1 tablespoon sugar
½ cup chopped pitted green olives
1 tablespoon drained capers
1 tablespoon chopped fresh parsley

Yields 24 small portions

In a large skillet, sauté the celery in the olive oil until soft and translucent, about 6 minutes. Remove the celery with a slotted spoon and set aside. Sauté the diced eggplant in the same pan until soft; remove from the pan and drain on paper towels to remove excess oil.

Sauté the onion in the same pan until soft.

In a small bowl, mix the tomato paste with the water. Add the mixture to the skillet along with the vinegar and sugar, and simmer for 15 minutes. Return the eggplant and celery to the pan and add the olives, capers, and parsley. Cook for 10 more minutes. Serve warm or cold.

PURÉE OF CHICK-PEAS
Puré di Ceci

Many years ago when I was consultant to a leading food packer, I made this cocktail dip to show them how versatile this bean is. Serve it with an assortment of fresh vegetables, crackers, or corn chips.

1 can (19 ounces) chick-peas (garbanzo beans), drained
2 teaspoons fresh lemon juice
1 clove garlic
½ teaspoon white pepper
1 teaspoon extra-virgin olive oil
Assorted raw vegetables and *Crostini* (see page 13)

Yields 2 cups

Combine the chick-peas, lemon juice, garlic, and pepper in a food processor or blender and purée into a smooth paste. Pour into a bowl and drizzle olive oil on top. Place bowl on a platter and arrange with cut vegetables and *crostini*.

Marinated Olives

Olive Marinate

In our house, marinated olives are a must when serving cold cuts.

1¼ pounds of your favorite cured olives
3 cloves garlic, crushed
1½ teaspoons dried thyme
2 dashes hot sauce
12 long strips lemon zest
1 teaspoon chopped Italian parsley
¾ cup extra-virgin olive oil
Freshly ground black pepper to taste

Combine all the ingredients in a container with a tight-fitting lid. Shake, shake, shake, and allow to marinate in the refrigerator for a few days or longer before serving.

It's a good idea to shake occasionally each day. When ready to serve, remove the olives from the container with a slotted spoon. Save the flavored oil for spreading on bread or to use as a vegetable dip. It is also good splashed over chicken before roasting.

TOAST

Crostini

In Italy, toasted slices of bread are used in so many ways. They hold delicate toppings (see Bruschetta, page 2). They may be crumbled into stews and soups or tossed into salads like croutons.

¼ **cup extra virgin olive oil**
1 **clove garlic, pressed**
½ **teaspoon dried basil**
18 **slices Italian bread, cut about ½ inch thick**

Yields 18 pieces

Preheat the oven to 350°F. In a small bowl, combine the oil, garlic, and basil. Brush the mixture on both sides of the bread and arrange the slices on a large baking sheet. Bake for 20 to 30 minutes, turning once, until both sides are golden tan. Serve warm.

TOMATOES WITH BASIL AND MOZZARELLA CHEESE

Pomodori con Basilico e Mozzarella (also Caprese)

This simplest of appetizers reinforces the adage that "less is more." Use the best and freshest possible ingredients here. Your tomatoes must be ripe, bursting with flavor.

4 large ripe tomatoes
Salt to taste (optional)
½ cup extra-virgin olive oil
1 cup shredded fresh basil, plus a few whole leaves for garnish (if fresh not available, use 1 tablespoon dried)
8 ounces mozzarella cheese, thinly sliced (freshly made is best)
Freshly ground black pepper to taste

Serves 6 to 8

Cut the tomatoes in half and scoop out the seeds. Sprinkle the tomatoes with salt and put on a plate with the cut sides down. Let stand for 20 to 30 minutes, then drain off the juices.

Cut the tomatoes into thick slices and arrange on a large serving platter. Drizzle with olive oil and then sprinkle with basil.

Arrange the mozzarella (near room temperature is best) over the tomatoes. Grind pepper over the mozzarella and garnish with whole basil leaves.

CHAPTER 2

Soups and Stews
Zuppe e Umidi

BROTH

Brodo

*M*any Italian recipes call for a good brodo, or broth. It is the main ingredient in zuppa, *soup,* or in the general category of minestra, *soups that have additional ingredients, the most famous being the hearty soup* minestrone *(see page 24).* Brodo *can be made with all chicken, as it is here, with all beef, or with beef and chicken together. Beef is sometimes referred to as brown stock, and chicken as white stock.*

The following is the broth I use the most and the one I remember Mom always having on hand. A pot of it always seemed to be cooking on the stove, and Dad, being a pretty good cook, would add his personal touch to the brewing brodo *when Mom wasn't looking. A bowl of* brodo *was the centerpiece of many a snack and a conversation in the kitchen.*

This broth freezes well in ice cube trays. Just pop a few into soups, sauces, whatever.

(continued)

3 pounds chicken, cut up
4½ quarts fresh cold water
2 large carrots, peeled
2 stalks celery
3 medium onions, peeled
2 bay leaves
1 tablespoon whole peppercorns
½ teaspoon dried marjoram
½ teaspoon dried thyme
Salt to taste (optional)

Yields 2 quarts

Wash the chicken parts, place them in a stockpot, and cover with the cold water. Coarsely cut up the vegetables and add to the pot. Add the bay leaves, peppercorns, marjoram, thyme, and salt.

Cover and bring to a boil, then lower the heat to a simmer. Occasionally skim off any foam from the surface. Continue to cook at a slow simmer, covered, for 2½ to 3 hours. Remove the cover and simmer an additional hour to concentrate all the flavors. Add boiling water if the stock level gets too low.

Strain the stock and skim off the fat. Save the tenderest chicken meat, but discard the skin, bones, and vegetables. Freeze the meat for use in other recipes.

ESCAROLE SOUP
Minestra di Scarola

Escarole is wonderful both raw, as a robust green salad vegetable, or cooked, especially in soups. The bold taste of this soup paves the way for a roast or other hearty main course.

1 large unpeeled potato, diced
6 cups chicken broth (recipe on page 15)
1 clove garlic, crushed
1 tablespoon fresh lemon juice
1½ pounds escarole, washed and chopped
1 tablespoon tomato paste
¼ teaspoon red pepper flakes, crushed
Freshly ground black pepper to taste
Salt to taste (optional)
¼ cup grated Romano cheese

Serves 4 to 6

Put the potato, broth, garlic, lemon juice, and escarole in a large saucepan, bring to a boil, and then reduce to a simmer. Add the tomato paste, red pepper flakes, black pepper, and salt. Continue to simmer until the potato is cooked. Mix in Romano cheese before serving.

ZUCCHINI SOUP

Minestra di Zucchini

Dad's large summer crop of zucchini led to many creative, tasty recipes. This soup has an intense flavor, and the wonderful perfume of tomatoes.

1 small onion, finely chopped
1 carrot, diced
1 clove garlic
1 tablespoon olive oil
1½ quarts chicken broth (recipe on page 15)
8 medium or 4 large zucchini, chopped
1 16-ounce can plum tomatoes, chopped
1 teaspoon dried thyme
1 tablespoon lemon juice
Salt to taste (optional)
Freshly grated black pepper to taste
1 cup small pasta, such as ditalini
½ cup grated Parmesan cheese

Serves 6

In a small skillet, sauté the onion, carrot, and garlic in the olive oil until soft.

Meanwhile, put the broth in large saucepan and add the zucchini, tomatoes, thyme, lemon juice, salt, and pepper. When the onion, carrot, and garlic are soft, add them to the broth.

Bring to a boil, then reduce to a simmer. Cover and cook for 35 to 40 minutes, then remove half the ingredients, including broth, and purée in a blender or food processor. Return to the pan and add the pasta and cheese. Continue to cook, covered, for an additional 15 minutes.

PRINCESS SOUP
Minestra Principessa

A simple, but delicious soup.

1 large egg
⅛ teaspoon freshly ground nutmeg
3 cups chicken broth (recipe on page 15)
Freshly ground black pepper to taste
1 tablespoon grated Parmesan cheese

Serves 4

Break the egg into a small bowl, add the nutmeg, and beat well with a wire whisk. Bring the chicken broth to a boil and pour in the egg, stirring constantly with the whisk. The egg will float in small pieces.

Pour the soup into individual serving bowls. Add a twist of ground pepper, sprinkle with Parmesan cheese, and serve.

CAULIFLOWER SOUP
Minestra di Cavolfiore

This hearty soup, filled with chunks of cauliflower, is a welcome sight on a cold night.

1 small cauliflower
1 small onion, finely chopped
¼ cup olive oil
2 quarts chicken broth (recipe on page 15)
1 teaspoon dried thyme
¼ teaspoon ground nutmeg
2 tablespoons tomato paste
1 cup ditali or other small pasta
Freshly ground black pepper to taste
Salt to taste (optional)
Grated Parmesan cheese

Serves 4 to 6

Wash the cauliflower thoroughly and break into small florets. In a large soup pot, sauté the onion in the olive oil until soft. Add the broth, cauliflower, thyme, nutmeg, and tomato paste and bring to a boil. Reduce to a simmer and cook, covered, for 45 minutes.

Stir in the pasta, pepper, and salt. Cook, uncovered, for approximately 15 minutes more.

Serve with grated Parmesan cheese.

UNCLE TONY'S LENTIL SOUP
Minestra di Lenticchie deuo Zio Antonio

Uncle Tony loved lentils and would make his very own pot of soup, which he shared only with me. I used to look forward to sitting down and chatting with him about his early days with my dad, his other brothers, and their one sister.

With apologies to Uncle Tony, I've taken the liberty of removing some fat from his recipe by using low-fat milk and eliminating the ton of dried pepperoni he would dice into the soup when Gran wasn't looking.

1½ cups dried lentils
1 to 2 ham hocks
6 cups water
2 carrots, diced
2 bay leaves
Freshly ground black pepper to taste
1 cup low-fat milk
Salt to taste (optional)

Serves 6 to 8; yields approximately 1½ quarts

Rinse the lentils and combine with all the other ingredients in large pot. Bring to a boil, then reduce the heat to a simmer. Cover and cook for 1½ hours, stirring occasionally.

Remove the ham hocks and pull off the meat, discarding the fat and bone. Return the meat to the pot and cook an additional hour.

FISH SOUP

Zuppa di Pesce

Use only the freshest fish in this recipe. You can vary the ingredients, depending upon what your fishmonger has on hand.

3 pounds assorted ocean fish, cleaned, with heads and tails left on
(cod, sea bass, snapper, halibut, haddock, monkfish)
1 pound shrimp
1 pound mussels
3 quarts water
2 onions, chopped
2 bay leaves
¼ teaspoon turmeric
4 stalks celery, chopped
1 teaspoon lemon juice
Freshly ground black pepper to taste
Salt to taste (optional)
Oil
3 cloves garlic, chopped
1 16-ounce can Italian plum tomatoes, chopped and drained
½ teaspoon dried thyme
1 teaspoon dried basil
½ teaspoon hot sauce
½ cup chopped Italian parsley

Serves 6 to 8

Cut the fish into large chunks, reserving the bones, heads, and tails. Shell the shrimp, reserving the shells. Soak and scrub the mussels. Refrigerate the fish, shrimp, and mussels.

Place the water in large stockpot, add the fish heads and tails, shrimp shells, onions, bay leaves, turmeric, celery, lemon juice, pepper, and salt. Bring to a boil, then reduce the heat and let simmer for 1½ hours.

Meanwhile, heat the oil in large skillet and sauté the garlic until soft. Add the tomatoes, thyme, basil, hot sauce, and parsley. Set aside.

When the stock is nearly finished, add the mussels and cook for 5 minutes or until the shells open. Remove the mussels with a slotted spoon and set aside. Strain the stock through cheesecloth. The stock should now be reduced to 2 quarts. Rinse the stockpot and return the stock to it. Mix in the garlic-tomato mixture, add the raw fish, and simmer approximately 30 minutes. Add the mussels during the last 15 minutes.

SPINACH SOUP
Minestra di Spinaci

Here's a way to serve your salad and soup in one course!

1½ pounds fresh spinach (or 2 10-ounce packages frozen), washed and chopped
6 cups chicken broth (recipe on page 15)
1 clove garlic, crushed
½ cup long-grain rice
½ teaspoon ground nutmeg
1 tablespoon fresh lemon juice
Freshly ground black pepper to taste
Salt to taste (optional)
¼ cup grated Romano cheese

Serves 4 to 6

If fresh spinach is used, it must be cleaned thoroughly and chopped. Place the broth, garlic, and spinach in a large saucepan. Bring to boil, then add the rice, nutmeg, lemon juice, pepper, and salt, and simmer until the rice is cooked but firm.

Serve hot and pass the Romano cheese and more pepper.

Crostini (page 13) make an ideal accompaniment.

VEGETABLE SOUP

Minestrone

This is a BIG hearty soup, chunky style, a meal in one dish. When we were kids, my brother and I would stand our spoons in it to see how long it would take them to fall over!

Although there are endless variations on this soup, this version is the one that got me to adulthood.

1 carrot, diced
1 leek, white only, thinly sliced
1 onion, finely chopped
2 stalks celery, diced
¼ cup olive oil
2 quarts water (broth can be used if desired)
1 cup dried white kidney beans, soaked for 6 to 8 hours or overnight, or 1 9-ounce can beans, undrained
1 potato, unpeeled, diced
1 small head Savoy cabbage, shredded fine
2 small zucchini, diced
1 tablespoon tomato paste
1 tablespoon chopped fresh parsley
½ teaspoon dried thyme
1 cup long-grain rice or small pasta
1 tablespoon Pesto (recipe on page 57) or 2 tablespoons dried basil and 2 tablespoons grated Parmesan cheese
Freshly ground black pepper to taste
Salt to taste (optional)

Serves 6

In a large stockpot, sauté the carrot, leek, onion, and celery in the olive oil for 5 minutes. Add the water or broth, soaked beans (if using canned beans, do *not* add now), potato, cabbage, zucchini, and tomato paste.

Bring to a boil, then reduce the heat to a simmer. Add the parsley and thyme, cover, and cook for 1¾ hours. Add the rice or pasta (and canned beans if using), pesto, pepper, and salt and simmer, uncovered, for an additional 30 minutes.

Serve with grated Parmesan cheese.

ROASTED CHESTNUT BISQUE
Passato di Catagne

W̌hen the executive producer of Live with Regis and Kathie Lee *challenged me to come up with a great New Year's dinner offering, I rose to the occasion and prepared this elegant soup. The flavor is marvelous and improves over time—make it a day ahead for an even richer taste.*

1 pound leeks, chopped, including ½ of green
2 tablespoons unsalted butter
1 small carrot, chopped
1 pound roasted fresh chestnuts, shelled
2½ cups concentrated turkey or chicken stock
¾ cup light cream
½ cup marsala
½ teaspoon white pepper
¼ teaspoon freshly ground nutmeg
Salt to taste (optional)
Approximately 4 ounces sour cream

Serves 6 to 8 small portions

In a large saucepan, sauté the leeks in the butter until soft. Add the carrot, chestnuts, and stock and simmer for 18 minutes or longer, until chestnuts are almost soft.

Place the mixture in a food processor or blender and purée until smooth. Return to the pan and add the light cream, marsala, white pepper, nutmeg, and salt. Simmer the soup over low heat, stirring continuously, for another 10 minutes.

When ready to serve, ladle into bowls and garnish with a dollop of sour cream.

BEAN BISQUE
Passato di Fagioli

As a little guy, I used to plead with my mother to make this hearty winter soup. To me, the savory taste of the velvety liquid was as good as dessert. Mom used dried beans, heavy cream, and eggs; I've modified my recipe and use canned beans and a much lighter broth.

1 onion, chopped
1 tablespoon extra-virgin olive oil
1 medium potato, unpeeled and chopped
1 carrot, chopped
3 cups beef broth
½ cup wine or sherry (optional)
1 19-ounce can *cannellini* (white kidney beans), undrained
1 8-ounce container plain low-fat yogurt
½ teaspoon ground white pepper
¼ teaspoon freshly ground nutmeg
Salt to taste (optional)
1 tablespoon chopped fresh parsley
Small lemon wedges

Serves 4 to 6

In a soup pot, sauté the onion in the olive oil until soft. Add the potato, carrot, and broth, bring to a boil, reduce to a simmer, and cook, covered, for 18 minutes, until the carrot and potato are fairly soft. Remove the pot from the heat and strain the soup, reserving the vegetables. Return the broth to the pot. Add wine.

Place the strained vegetables and the cannellini in a food processor or blender and purée. Add the purée to the broth, then stir in the yogurt, pepper, nutmeg, and salt. Simmer, uncovered, for several minutes, until the flavors are well blended. Sprinkle with chopped parsley and serve with lemon wedges.

PUMPKIN SOUP
Minestra di Zucca

This soup is everything a rich, velvety soup should be, and it also features the unusual taste of pumpkin. If you've never tasted pumpkin this way, you'll be pleasantly surprised.

6 shallots, peeled and chopped
2 tablespoons unsalted butter
3 cups chicken broth (recipe on page 15)
½ cup *acini di pepe* pasta (very small, resembles rice)
1½ cups canned pumpkin
½ cup light cream
3 tablespoons grated Parmesan cheese
⅓ cup chopped fresh dill
½ teaspoon dry mustard
Freshly ground black pepper to taste
Salt to taste (optional)

Serves 6 to 8

In a large saucepan, cook the shallots in the butter until soft. Add the broth, bring to a boil, and add the pasta. Continue to cook about 5 minutes.

Stir in the pumpkin, cream, and grated Parmesan. Reduce the heat to a simmer, and add the dill, mustard, pepper, and salt. Continue to cook over low heat for about 25 minutes. Serve hot.

Egg-Marsala Soup

Ginestrata

Many a day my Aunt Rose would make this wonderful soup. She claimed her doctor had recommended the marsala wine and egg for her "anemic condition" (a surprising diagnosis for such a robust-looking woman).

Aunt Rose figured that if a little marsala was good, more should be better. But she didn't waste it in the soup, where the alcohol would evaporate when cooked. Instead, she sipped it from a shot glass kept atop the stove. As she cooked and sipped, she also sang opera. Aunt Rose was a wonderful cook—I cannot say the same for her singing.

5 large egg yolks
½ cup dry marsala
1 teaspoon ground cinnamon
3 cups chicken broth (recipe on page 15), chilled
¼ cup unsalted butter, softened
1 teaspoon sugar
¼ teaspoon ground nutmeg

Serves 4

In a large bowl, beat the egg yolks and slowly add the marsala while still beating. Add the cinnamon and broth, beating all the while. Strain.

Place this mixture in a double boiler. Cook over medium heat and stir in the butter little by little. The soup should *never* boil, but right before that point you should remove it from the heat and pour into warm small soup bowls.

Combine the sugar and nutmeg and sprinkle on top of the soup. Serve immediately.

RIBOLLITA

As we've all discovered, leftover hearty dishes often taste even better the next day. This dish serves as proof; hence the Italian name Ribollita *which translates as "Reboiled." Use leftover* minestrone.

1 recipe for *minestrone* soup (page 24)
8 to 12 slices *crostini*
Grated Parmesan cheese

Serves 4 to 6

Reheat the leftover *minestrone*. Place *crostini* in the bottom of each serving bowl and pour soup over them; layer more *crostini* and pour in more soup.

Cover and let stand for a minute or two, then with a large spoon, break up the bread slices and mix altogether. Sprinkle with Parmesan cheese and serve.

CHAPTER 3

🐘

Salads, Sauces, and Dressings
Insalate, Salse, e Condimenti

*F*resh, leafy green salads, full of life, were always a part of Mom's meals. The dressings were always made with pure fruity olive oil and our neighbor's homemade wine vinegar.

Today, more options are available with balsamic vinegars, light olive oils, and a variety of fresh, flavorful herbs that weren't available in most supermarkets even ten years ago.

I've included salads in this section that are almost meals in themselves, like string bean and potato salad; refreshing starters like Mom's orange salad, and salads to be served as a satisfying end of the meal, like radicchio and arugula.

There are also some great side salads like Cousin Teresa's potato salad for light meals, picnics, and buffets.

Sauces always bring out the artist in the Italian cook. Pesto is one of my favorites. It turns an ordinary piece of broiled chicken into a sensation, and is great on bread or on baked potatoes. I also mix it with ricotta for filled pasta and top it with my pink or white sauce. A dish fit for Leonardo.

STRING BEANS AND POTATO SALAD

Fagiolini e Patate all'Agro

1½ pounds small red Bliss potatoes
8 ounces string beans
¼ cup olive oil
2 tablespoons balsamic vinegar
1 clove garlic, minced
½ small red onion, finely chopped
Salt to taste (optional)
Freshly grated black pepper to taste

Serves 4 to 6

In a large saucepan, cook the potatoes with their skins on until tender. Drain and cut them into quarters. In a medium saucepan, cook the beans until they turn bright green and are just tender. Remove from the heat and plunge the beans into cold water (this stops the cooking process and keeps them firm). Place the potatoes and beans in large serving bowl and set aside.

In a small bowl, combine the oil, vinegar, garlic, onion, salt, and pepper. Gently toss with the potatoes and beans.

Serve at room temperature or cover and refrigerate before serving.

RADICCHIO AND ARUGULA SALAD

Insalata di Radicchio e Arugula

In this great-looking, great-tasting salad, radicchio and arugula offer a pungent start or finish to a meal. Arugula's dark green leaves have a peppery taste, while radicchio's red leaves are slightly bitter. Serve your salad the Italian way, after the main course.

1 head radicchio
1 bunch arugula
Balsamic Vinaigrette (recipe on page 40)
Freshly ground black pepper to taste

Serves 4 to 6

Wash the radicchio and arugula thoroughly and dry. Tear the radicchio into bite-size pieces and combine with the arugula. Add the dressing, toss, and serve. Add ground pepper.

BREAD AND TOMATO SALAD
Panzanella

This Florentine recipe requires good crusty Italian bread. Tuscan, of course, is ideal! The tomatoes should be bursting with ripeness for this simple but satisfying salad.

½ loaf crusty Italian bread, cut into cubes
2 ripe tomatoes, cut into cubes
1 medium red onion, chopped
½ cup extra-virgin olive oil
1 tablespoon balsamic vinegar
¼ cup chopped fresh basil
Freshly ground black pepper to taste
Salt to taste (optional)

Serves 6

In a large bowl, combine the bread, tomatoes, and onion. In a separate bowl, mix the oil, vinegar, basil, pepper, and salt. Add the dressing to the bread and tomato mixture and toss lightly. Let stand 15 to 20 minutes, toss lightly again, and serve.

CAESAR SALAD

This salad was not created for or named after the Emperor Caesar. In fact, it's said to be the creation of a waiter in Italy whose first name, of course, was Caesar. He used it to impress his guests with his table-side showmanship. Now, just like Caesar, you can impress guests in your own home.

I recommend that you prepare fresh croutons. Of course, store-bought can be used, but try to find an unseasoned variety.

1 head romaine lettuce
2 cloves garlic, peeled
¼ cup extra virgin olive oil
6 anchovy fillets, rinsed
1 large egg, coddled
Juice of 1 lemon
½ teaspoon dry mustard
1 tablespoon Worcestershire sauce
Dash or 2 hot sauce
Dash bitters
¼ cup grated Romano or Parmesan cheese
Freshly ground black pepper to taste
1½ cups croutons (recipe follows)
Salt to taste (optional)

Serves 4 to 6

Wash the romaine, dry thoroughly, and tear into bite-size pieces.

In a large wooden salad bowl, mash the garlic with a little olive oil. Using a spoon, swirl and paint the interior of the bowl with the crushed garlic and oil, pressing it into the surface of the bowl. Add the anchovy fillets and mash with the oil and garlic. Prepare egg in water just below the boiling point for 2 minutes. Add the egg, lemon juice, mustard, Worcestershire sauce, hot sauce, bitters, and 2 teaspoons of the cheese. Finally, add the rest of the olive oil and whip until the dressing is creamy. Let stand for a few minutes.

Whip the dressing again and add the romaine. Toss with the dressing, making sure to cover each leaf. Sprinkle with the remainder of the cheese and grind on fresh pepper. Add the croutons and toss again. Salt and serve immediately.

GARLIC CROUTONS
2 tablespoons olive oil
2 tablespoons butter
2 cloves garlic crushed
6 slices Italian or French bread
Freshly ground black pepper to taste

Yields approximately 3 cups

Preheat the oven to 325°F. In a medium skillet, heat the oil, butter, and pepper. Add the garlic and sauté until it is golden. Discard the garlic and remove the skillet from the heat.

Brush the slices of bread on both sides with the butter and oil mixture. Place the bread on a large cookie sheet and bake 15 to 20 minutes, or until golden brown and crisp. When cool, cut into cubes.

Store in a covered container in the refrigerator.

COUSIN TERESA'S POTATO SALAD

Patate all'Agro della Cugina Teresa

In every Italian family, relatives have signature dishes. Aunt Rose has her egg and marsala soup, Uncle Tony has his pasta cake, and cousin Teresa has her potato salad. It's nothing like the thick, gloppy potato salad from the store. Cousin Teresa's slightly pungent dressing doesn't mask the flavor of the potatoes.

8 potatoes, peeled and sliced
1 cup fresh or frozen peas
1 bunch scallions, sliced
1 stalk celery, diced
1 tablespoon Dijon mustard
1 tablespoon cider vinegar
1 cup low-fat mayonnaise
1 teaspoon sugar
1 teaspoon white pepper
¼ teaspoon turmeric

Serves 4 to 6

Place the potatoes in a stockpot, cover with water, and bring to a boil. Cook for 15 minutes, then add the peas and continue cooking until the vegetables are tender but not soft. Drain in a colander and let cool.

In a large bowl, combine potatoes and peas with the scallions and celery.

In a small bowl, mix the mustard, vinegar, mayonnaise, sugar, pepper, and turmeric. Add to the vegetables and toss.

STRING BEAN SALAD

Fagiolini all'Agro

My mother loves to serve this salad on hot summer evenings along with slices of cold chicken or a simply done fresh fish entrée. Add chilled white wine, crusty bread, and a bowl of fruit, and you've got the perfect summer meal.

1 pound string beans
¼ cup olive oil
2 tablespoons balsamic vinegar
1 clove garlic, minced
½ small red onion, minced
Freshly ground black pepper to taste
Salt to taste (optional)
1 hard-boiled egg white, chopped

Serves 4 to 6

Place the beans in a large saucepan with a small amount of water and blanch until they are bright green. When done, plunge the beans into cold water to discontinue the cooking process and to keep them firm.

In a large bowl, combine the oil, vinegar, garlic, onion, pepper, and salt. Add the beans and toss. Cover and refrigerate for a few hours.

Before serving, sprinkle chopped egg white on top.

Garden Salad

Insalata dell'Orto

The traditional Italian kitchen always has an assortment of fresh vegetables on hand. This salad puts many of them to good use.

⅓ head chicory, torn into bite-size pieces
⅓ head escarole, torn into bite-size pieces
⅓ head romaine lettuce, torn into bite-size pieces
½ head endive, torn into bite-size pieces
½ cup diced tomatoes
½ cup small broccoli florets
½ cup diced fennel (*finocchio*)
½ cup small cauliflower florets
½ cup diced carrots
1 tablespoon drained capers
½ cup pitted and chopped black olives
1½-inch-thick slice salami, cut into thin strips
1½-inch-thick slice provolone cheese, cut into thin strips
Balsamic Vinaigrette (recipe on page 40)

Serves 6 to 8

In a large bowl, toss the ingredients with balsamic vinaigrette or another dressing of your choice.

THERESA'S ORANGE SALAD

Aranci alla Theresa

When I was growing up, holiday meals in our house always began with my mother's orange salad. This simple but delicious dish heralded the many courses to come. As children, my brother and I thought this salad was very strange. Today we make salads with every conceivable kind of fruit, and it is "très chic" and healthy! Although I list the anchovies as an option, tasting them with orange is a delightful experience.

4 large navel oranges, peeled
18 medium black olives, pitted (you may use canned)
Anchovy fillets, rinsed (optional)
¼ cup extra–virgin olive oil
Sprigs of Italian parsley
Salt to taste (optional)
Freshly ground black pepper to taste

Serves 8

Slice the oranges about ¼ inch thick and arrange on a serving platter. Place a whole olive in the center of each orange slice. Add anchovy fillets atop several orange slices. Drizzle with olive oil and let the salad stand approximately 20 minutes.

Tuck sprigs of parsley between the slices and sprinkle with salt and freshly ground pepper.

STUFFED CHERRY TOMATOES
Pomodori Ripieni

If you don't want to make your own pesto, try one of the kinds that supermarkets are now carrying in their refrigerator cases.

12 large cherry tomatoes, stems removed
⅓ cup ricotta cheese
1 tablespoon Pesto (recipe on page 57)
Freshly ground black pepper to taste
Minced fresh Italian parsley, for garnish

Yields 24 pieces

Cut the tomatoes in half and drain; remove the seeds, using small spoon if necessary.

Mix the ricotta, pesto, and pepper together. Fill the tomatoes generously and garnish with parsley.

BALSAMIC VINAIGRETTE
Vinagrette All'Aceto Balsamico

Balsamic vinegar is aged in casks, which is how it achieves its time-honored sweet-mellow flavor. Not only does it perk up a salad, but it is also a creative addition to many sauces.

Dress your greens in a large bowl rather than on individual salad plates. You'll use less dressing that way.

¾ cup extra-virgin olive oil
¼ cup balsamic vinegar
2 tablespoons Dijon mustard
1 teaspoon salt
⅛ teaspoon white pepper
1 medium clove garlic, crushed
½ teaspoon sugar
1 tablespoon water

Yields about 1¼ cups

Blend all the ingredients thoroughly. Store in a covered jar in the refrigerator. Shake well before using.

GREEN SAUCE
Salsa Verde

Here is a great sauce for serving with meats and fish, not pasta. A mini-food processor makes quick work of this sauce, but a mortar and pestle work just as well.

1 cup chopped fresh Italian parsley
1 cup bread crumbs
1 small clove garlic
2 anchovy fillets
1 tablespoon drained capers
2 tablespoons fresh lemon juice
Freshly ground black pepper to taste
½ cup olive oil

Yields approximately 1¼ cups

In a food processor or blender, process all the ingredients except the olive oil; then, with the machine still running, add the olive oil in a slow, steady stream. Float a thin layer of olive oil on top to prevent discoloring.

Store in the refrigerator, but bring to room temperature before serving.

WHITE SAUCE
Salsa Besciamella

Filled pastas, such as cannelloni and lasagne, are sometimes topped with a white sauce. This medium white sauce can be made thicker or thinner depending on the amount of flour used. If you don't want a stark white sauce, add a tiny drop of yellow food coloring.

For a truly rich sauce, substitute heavy cream for the milk.

¼ **cup (½ stick) unsalted butter**
¼ **cup all-purpose flour**
2 cups 1% low-fat milk
⅛ **teaspoon grated nutmeg**
⅛ **teaspoon white pepper**
Salt to taste (optional)
1 drop yellow food coloring (optional)

Yields approximately 2¼ cups

In a small saucepan, melt the butter. Add flour, whisk, and then slowly add the milk. Simmer for 12 to 15 minutes, until thickened. Remove from the heat, and whisk in the nutmeg, pepper, salt, and food coloring.

PINK SAUCE WITH CHEESE
Salsa Rosa al Formaggio

This sauce can also be used for manicotti, cannelloni, and vegetables. Not only does it have great flavor, but it's good-looking!

1 recipe White Sauce (page 42)
2 tablespoons tomato sauce
½ cup grated Parmesan cheese
⅛ teaspoon white pepper

Yields about 3 cups

In a small saucepan, mix all the ingredients together and heat until the cheese melts and the sauce is blended.

PESTO SOUR CREAM
Panna Acida al Pesto

This is an unusual party dip, as well as a nice topping for baked potatoes. Yogurt can replace the sour cream if you like.

8 ounces low-fat sour cream
1 tablespoon Pesto (recipe on page 57)

Yields 1 cup

In a small bowl, mix the sour cream and pesto thoroughly.

PESTO CREAM SAUCE
Salsa alla Panna e Pesto

This sauce is delicious and easy! Toss with your favorite pasta or use as a sauce over manicotti or ravioli.

¼ **cup Pesto (recipe on page 57)**
½ **cup heavy cream**

Yields ¾ cup, enough for four 2-ounce servings of pasta

In a small saucepan, mix the pesto with the cream and heat while cooking your pasta.

PESTO RICOTTA CHEESE
Ricotta al Pesto

Fill your pastas with this ricotta or layer it into your lasagne. It's our secret!

8 ounces ricotta cheese (low-fat or no-fat)
1 tablespoon Pesto (recipe on page 57)

Yields 1 cup

In a small bowl, mix the ricotta and pesto thoroughly.

Pesto Olive Oil

Olio al Pesto

Pesto olive oil is an indispensable ingredient in any kitchen. I especially like to brush it on broiled meats and fish. It is a great dipping sauce for vegetables and bread.

¾ cup olive oil
1 tablespoon Pesto (recipe on page 57)

Yields ¾ cup

Place the olive oil and pesto in a covered jar and shake well, before using. Store in refrigerator

Pesto Butter

Burro al Pesto

Here is a great way to flavor everyday fare. I like it on everything from toast to potatoes.

¼ pound (1 stick) unsalted butter, softened
1 teaspoon Pesto (recipe on page 57)

Yields ½ cup

In a small bowl, cream the butter and pesto together.

CHAPTER 4

❧

Pasta and Polenta

Pasta e Polenta

PASTA

*T*here are so many pasta shapes and sizes that for a long time certain manufacturers put numbers on their packages to make a specific cut more easily identifiable. Many a time Mom sent me to the store and gave me a piece of paper with a number on it for the pasta I was to buy.

Today I notice that many supermarkets stock only the more popular cuts, such as spaghetti, linguine, ziti, rotelle, and penne. However, do look for and sample other cuts, like shells. If you were to cook various pastas with a different sauce every night, it would be years before you'd run out of recipes.

Spaghetti, linguine, and fettuccine are great for sauces that cling, while shaped pastas such as ziti, penne, and shells are ideal with vegetables and beans. And the tiniest shapes—ditalini, acini di pepe, and pastina—are wonderful additions to soups, stews, and chowders. Although they are all made with flour and water, each shape adds it own unique character to a particular sauce or topping.

Dried pasta, the type you find on supermarket shelves, is easy to store and easy to cook correctly. For each pound of pasta, start with 6 quarts of fresh cold water in a large covered pot. The water must be boiling before you add the pasta. (I do not add the traditional 2 tablespoons of salt to the boiling water.) You should add the pasta gradually to the boiling water in order to maintain the water temperature. Cover the pot until the water comes to a boil again, then remove the cover and add a teaspoon of olive oil, which will keep the pasta from sticking.

Stir frequently, and cook until the pasta is firm yet tender—al dente, which literally translates as "to the tooth." And that's what you must do—bite a piece during cooking to test the firmness. Remember, each shape has a different length of cooking time. Fresh pasta, as opposed to dried, cooks much more quickly, but remember that most fresh pasta also contains eggs. When pasta is cooked, you must be ready to serve it almost immediately.

When measuring the quantity of dried pasta for cooking, a good rule of thumb is 2 ounces of raw pasta for an appetizer portion and 3 to 4 ounces for a main course. And finally, remember that dried pasta expands when cooked, while fresh pasta does not.

LITTLE BITS OF PASTA
Pastina

When my brother and I were babies, our mom served us pastina instead of pablum. She'd either toss small bits of pasta into chicken soup broth or boil it along with an egg. I still crave pastina when I need a soothing treat.

1 quart chicken broth (recipe on page 15)
8 ounces pastina or alphabet pasta
2 large egg whites
2 tablespoons grated Parmesan cheese
Freshly ground black pepper to taste (optional)

Serves 4 to 6

In a medium saucepan, bring the broth to a boil and add the pastina. When almost done, add the egg whites and quickly stir. When al dente, serve with cheese and freshly ground pepper.

LENTILS WITH PASTA

Pasta e Lenticchie

The prosciutto ham lends a rich, savory taste to this hearty soup. Perfect for lunch.

1 tablespoon olive oil
½ slice prosciutto ham, ¼ inch thick, chopped
1 medium onion, chopped
2 cloves garlic
1 stalk celery, chopped
1 quart water
1 quart chicken broth (recipe on page 15)
8 ounces dried lentils (soaked overnight and drained)
1½ teaspoons tomato paste
Freshly ground black pepper to taste
Salt to taste (optional)
¾ cup small pasta, such as shells or ditalini
Grated Parmesan cheese
Red pepper flakes (optional)

Serves 4 to 6

Heat the olive oil in a medium skillet, then add the prosciutto, onion, garlic, and celery and sauté until soft. Add the water, broth, lentils, tomato paste, black pepper, and salt. Bring to a boil, then reduce to a simmer. Cook about 1½ to 2 hours; during the last 20 minutes of cooking, add the pasta. Sprinkle with Parmesan cheese and red pepper flakes, and serve.

PEAS AND SHELLS
Conchiglie ai Piselli

As children, my brother and I would use our Conchiglie ai Piselli *for a little game called "count the peas." My brother would always win, for while he was counting peas, I was eating my pasta—and his.*

8 ounces medium pasta shells
10 ounces frozen peas
½ cup chopped mushrooms
2 tablespoons water
2 cups cooked marinara sauce (recipe on page 67)
Grated Parmesan cheese
Freshly grated black pepper to taste
Salt to taste (optional)

Serves 4

Cook the pasta as usual (see page 47). Meanwhile, place the peas and mushrooms in a medium saucepan along with the water and steam until tender.

When the water evaporates, add the tomato sauce and heat through.

Drain the pasta, place in a serving bowl, and ladle the sauce over the top. Sprinkle with Parmesan cheese, pepper, and salt and serve.

PASTA WITH BROCCOLI
Pasta ai Broccoli

The hallmark of Italian cooking is elegant simplicity, and this intensely flavorful dish is a great example of why this Mediterranean cuisine is so popular. Try making the dish with extra-virgin olive oil; you'll taste the difference.

1 head broccoli
½ cup olive oil
1 large red bell pepper, seeded and cut into thin strips
2 cloves garlic, peeled
½ cup water
½ cup dry white wine
1 pound fettuccine or linguine
¼ cup unsalted butter
¾ cup grated Parmesan cheese
Freshly ground black pepper to taste
Salt to taste (optional)

Serves 4 to 6

Trim the leaves and rough ends from each stalk of broccoli and peel the skin with a vegetable peeler. Cut the stalks into 1-inch pieces and the head into small florets.

Heat the olive oil over moderate heat in a large skillet. Add the broccoli, red pepper strips, and garlic and cook for 1 minute, stirring frequently. Discard the garlic when golden. Add the water and wine, cover, and cook over low heat until the broccoli is just tender but firm, about 5 minutes.

Cook the pasta as usual (see page 47). Drain, return to the saucepan, and toss with the butter. Stir in the broccoli mixture, cheese, pepper, and salt.

SPRINGTIME PASTA
Pasta Primavera

I think of cooking as an art form, not a set of commandments, so this recipe can be your own creation. I've included some of my favorite ingredients and I expect you to do the same. I suggest, however, that you use extra virgin olive oil. It does make a "divine" difference!

Plan to cook the pasta while the vegetables are roasting, timing it so that pasta and vegetables are ready at the same time.

2 red onions, thickly sliced
1 red bell pepper, seeded and cut into strips
1 yellow bell pepper, seeded and cut into strips
1 purple bell pepper, seeded and cut into strips
2 baby eggplants, cut into chunks
1 yellow zucchini, cut into thick slices
1 green zucchini, cut into thick slices
¼ cup extra-virgin olive oil
1 tablespoon balsamic vinegar
1 teaspoon dried thyme
½ teaspoon dried basil
4 cloves garlic, peeled and crushed
Freshly ground black pepper to taste
Salt to taste (optional)
12 ounces penne, ziti, or other tubular pasta
2 tablespoons freshly grated Parmesan cheese
¼ cup chopped fresh Italian parsley
⅛ teaspoon red pepper flakes (optional)

Serves 6 as an appetizer or 3 to 4 as a main course

Preheat the oven to 425°F. In a large bowl, toss the vegetables with the olive oil, vinegar, thyme, basil, garlic, black pepper, and salt. Place the mixture on a cookie sheet or in a roasting pan and roast in the oven for about 30 minutes. Then place the pan under the broiler for 2 to 3 minutes, until edges of the vegetables become charred.

While the vegetables are roasting, begin cooking the pasta (see page 47). Transfer the vegetables to a serving bowl. Take about ½ cup of the water in which the pasta is cooking and add it to the vegetables. Then add the cheese, parsley, and red pepper flakes. Drain the pasta, toss with the vegetables, and serve.

PASTA WITH (DOUBLE) CHICK-PEAS

Pasta e Ceci, Ceci

This recipe is aptly named, since the chick-peas inject protein and flavor, but no fat.

2 cloves garlic
2 tablespoons extra virgin olive oil
2 16-ounce cans chick-peas with their liquid
1 cup chicken broth (recipe on page 15)
1 tablespoon tomato paste
1 teaspoon dried rosemary
Freshly grated black pepper to taste
Salt to taste (optional)
8 ounces shaped pasta such as elbows or shells
Grated Parmesan cheese

Serves 4 to 6

In a medium saucepan, sauté the garlic in the olive oil until golden. Add the chick-peas, broth, tomato paste, rosemary, pepper, and salt.

Bring to a boil, then reduce to a simmer. Cook for 20 to 30 minutes. As the ingredients cook, crush several chick-peas with a wooden spoon and stir.

Meanwhile, cook the pasta as usual (see page 47). Drain well, reserving 1 cup of the pasta water.

Stir the pasta into the chick-pea mixture and dilute with the reserved pasta water if desired. Sprinkle with Parmesan cheese and serve.

PENNE PASTA WITH PROSCIUTTO SAUCE

Pasta al Prosciutto

I first introduced this recipe on Live with Regis and Kathie Lee. *Kathie Lee raved that it was the best dish she'd ever tasted.*

8 ounces penne
3 tablespoons unsalted butter
4 ounces prosciutto, cut into strips ¼ inch wide
1 small onion, diced
6 plum tomatoes, diced
1 cup heavy cream
½ cup fresh or frozen peas
Freshly ground black pepper to taste
¼ cup grated Parmesan cheese

Serves 4 as an appetizer or 2 as a main course

Cook the pasta as usual (see page 47).

Meanwhile, in a large skillet, heat the butter over medium heat. Add the prosciutto and onion and cook for 3 to 5 minutes, until the onion is soft. Stir in the tomatoes. Add the cream, peas, and pepper and simmer until the mixture is slightly thickened. Add the Parmesan cheese and mix thoroughly. Toss with the pasta and serve.

PENNE WITH GOAT CHEESE

Pasta al Formaggio di Capra

Strong-flavored cheese is an acquired taste, but that doesn't mean it can't be a crowd pleaser! Goat cheese is turning up roasted on the best salad plates in town. Here I've teamed it up with ripe plum tomatoes for a robust pasta sauce.

1 pound penne
2 tablespoons extra virgin olive oil
6 plum tomatoes, chopped
6 ounces goat cheese
2 tablespoons chopped fresh basil
½ teaspoon dried thyme
Freshly grated black pepper to taste

Serves 4 to 6

Cook the pasta as usual (see page 47).

Meanwhile, in a medium skillet, heat the olive oil and add the tomatoes. Sauté until soft, then add the goat cheese; blend together and add the basil, thyme, and pepper.

Toss with the drained pasta and serve immediately.

PASTA WITH LOVE
Pasta con Amore

I developed this recipe for my performance at the 1992 Taste of Buffalo show. The official tasters loved it. It's easy, fast, and a real crowd pleaser.

12 ounces ziti or penne
2 bunches scallions, chopped
1 small red bell pepper, seeded and chopped
1 very large ripe tomato, chopped
½ cup olive oil
2 tablespoons drained capers
2 tablespoons chopped fresh basil (or 1 tablespoon dried basil)
2 cups (approximately) ricotta cheese (low-fat or no-fat)
Freshly ground black pepper to taste
Salt to taste (optional)
4 ounces mozzarella cheese, shredded (low-fat or no-fat)

Serves 4

Cook the pasta as usual (see page 47).

Meanwhile, in a medium saucepan, sauté the scallions, red pepper, and tomato in the olive oil until soft. Add the capers and basil and continue stirring. Then add the ricotta. Add pepper and salt. (If a smooth sauce is desired, put the ricotta through a fine strainer or sieve before adding to the pan.) Simmer until all the ingredients are blended together.

Divide the pasta among 4 plates and top with the sauce. Sprinkle with mozzarella and serve immediately.

PESTO

You can make this wonderful summer sauce easily in a food processor. Borrow one if need be, but forget about using a blender. If you freeze pesto into cubes in an ice cube tray, you will always have a little to enjoy in recipes whenever needed.

This heady, basil-infused concentrate goes a long way. A teaspoon of pesto adds zest to cold gazpacho or similar soups. And as you will see in the recipes on the pages that follow, pesto enlivens stuffing-filled pastas, lasagnes, and cocktail party dips. I also like to thin it with olive oil and use it on baked, broiled, or grilled meats, chicken, or fish.

1½ to 2 cups loosely packed basil leaves
¼ cup Italian parsley leaves
2 tablespoons walnut pieces
1 tablespoon pine nuts (*pignoli*)
1 clove garlic or more, to taste
3 tablespoons unsalted butter
¼ teaspoon white pepper
Pinch freshly grated nutmeg
¼ teaspoon grated orange peel
½ cup grated Parmesan cheese or 4 ounces, cut up
3 ounces olive oil or more if needed

Yields about 1½ cups

Wash and dry the basil and parsley leaves. Blanch the walnuts and pine nuts (a quick dip approximately 30 seconds in boiling water).

Place the steel blade in a food processor. Add the walnuts, pine nuts, garlic, butter, pepper, nutmeg, and orange peel. With the machine running, add the cheese through the feed tube. Add the basil and parsley through the tube and process until you have a thick paste.

With the machine still running, slowly and steadily trickle the olive oil through the tube and continue processing until the pesto is smooth.

To serve over hot pasta, dilute the pesto with 1 tablespoon of the pasta cooking water per portion and toss with the hot pasta. Additional pasta water can be added if a thinner consistency is desired. About 1 tablespoon of pesto to 2 ounces of pasta is average for a serving, since this is a concentrated sauce.

PASTA WITH WHITE CLAM SAUCE

Pasta al Sugo Bianco di Vongole

Have plenty of crusty Italian bread to soak up and savor the subtle taste of fresh clams gently seasoned and coaxed into a sauce.

2 pounds cherrystone clams (approximately 24 clams)
12 ounces linguine or vermicelli
1 clove garlic, crushed
¼ cup olive oil
2 tablespoons unsalted butter
1 cup bottled clam juice
½ cup white wine
⅛ teaspoon white pepper
1 teaspoon fresh lemon juice
1 tablespoon chopped fresh Italian parsley
Salt to taste (optional)

Serves 4 as an appetizer or 2 to 3 as a main course

Wash the clams thoroughly, place in a large saucepan with a little water, cover, and steam until they open. Remove the clams with a slotted spoon, then strain the pan juices and set aside. Remove the clams from their shells, discarding the brown sac in each clam. Chop the flesh and set aside.

Begin cooking the pasta as usual (see page 47). Meanwhile, in a medium skillet, sauté the garlic in the olive oil and discard when golden. Add the butter, reserved clam juice, bottled clam juice, white wine, and pepper.

Simmer 5 to 8 minutes, then add the clams, lemon juice, parsley, and salt and cook an additional 3 minutes. Toss with the pasta and serve.

PASTA WITH RED CLAM SAUCE
Pasta alle Vongole

To those purists who think that clams have no place in tomato sauce, forgive me! But I'd be remiss if I didn't share this old family favorite, laden with the sweet taste of tender clams.

2 pounds cherrystone clams (approximately 24 clams)
1 clove garlic, crushed
¼ cup olive oil
2 tablespoons unsalted butter
2 cups drained canned tomatoes, crushed
1 cup bottled clam juice
½ cup white wine
⅛ teaspoon dried thyme
⅛ teaspoon white pepper
12 ounces linguine or vermicelli
1 teaspoon fresh lemon juice
1 tablespoon chopped fresh parsley
Salt to taste (optional)

Serves 4 as an appetizer or 2 to 3 as a main course

Wash the clams thoroughly, place in a large saucepan with a little water, cover, and steam until they open. Remove the clams with a slotted spoon, then strain the pan juices and set aside. Remove the clams from their shells, discarding the brown sac in each clam. Chop the flesh and set aside.

In a medium skillet, sauté the garlic in the olive oil and discard when golden. Add the butter, tomatoes, reserved clam juice, bottled clam juice, white wine, thyme, and pepper and simmer 12 to 15 minutes.

While the sauce is simmering, cook the pasta as usual (see page 47). Then add the clams, lemon juice, parsley, and salt to the sauce and cook an additional 3 minutes. Toss with the pasta and serve.

SPAGHETTI AND TUNA

Spaghetti al Tonno

When a simple can of tuna is paired with plum tomatoes, the result is this easy, tasty dish.

2 tablespoons olive oil
2 tablespoons unsalted butter
1 clove garlic
1 28-ounce can Italian plum tomatoes, drained and coarsely chopped
1 6⅛-ounce can tuna in vegetable oil, drained
Freshly ground black pepper to taste
12 ounces spaghetti or linguine
Sprigs of Italian parsley for garnish

Serves 4

In a medium skillet, heat the olive oil and butter, add the garlic and tomatoes, and sauté for 20 minutes. Remove the garlic when golden. Add the tuna to the skillet and break it apart with a fork. Cook over low heat for 10 minutes and add pepper to taste.

Cook the spaghetti or linguine as usual (see page 47). Serve the sauce over the pasta and garnish with parsley sprigs.

LINGUINE WITH ANCHOVIES

Linguine alle Acciughe

I now know why I loved this simple dish as a child. I love anchovies. To this day, whenever I am making a recipe that calls for anchovies, I always have extra on the side for me.

If you are using canned anchovies, rinse the fillets to remove some of the salt and discard the oil in which they are packed.

1 pound linguine
1 cup olive oil
2 cloves garlic
8 anchovy fillets, chopped
8 black olives, chopped
2½ cups plain bread crumbs
½ cup chopped fresh Italian parsley
Freshly ground black pepper to taste
Red pepper flakes, crushed (optional)

Serves 4 as a main course or 6 to 8 as an appetizer

Begin cooking the pasta in the usual way (see page 47).

Meanwhile, heat ½ cup of the oil in a medium skillet, sauté the garlic until golden, and discard. Remove the skillet from the heat and add the anchovies. Mix them into the oil to dissolve into a sauce.

In another skillet, heat the remaining oil and add the olives and bread crumbs. Cook until the bread crumbs are a golden tan.

Drain the pasta and immediately bathe in the anchovy sauce. Top individual servings of the pasta with the bread crumb mixture. Sprinkle with parsley and pepper and red pepper flakes. Serve immediately.

Fettuccine with Peas in Cheese Sauce

Fettuccine con Piselli Formaggio

This creamy sauce is especially good with the wide fettuccine noodle, but of course other pasta can be substituted.

1 pound fresh or dried fettuccine
½ cup unsalted butter
½ cup fresh or frozen peas
½ cup sliced mushrooms
½ cup light cream
½ cup grated Parmesan cheese
Freshly ground black pepper to taste
Salt to taste (optional)

Serves 4

Begin cooking the pasta as usual (see page 47).

Meanwhile, in a medium skillet, melt the butter over low heat. Add the peas and mushrooms and cook over low heat for about 3 minutes. Add the cream to the skillet, stirring constantly, and cook until it thickens, about 5 minutes. Add the Parmesan, pepper, and salt and cook another 2 to 3 minutes.

Drain the pasta and toss with the sauce.

LINGUINE AMATRICE STYLE

Linguine all'Amatriciana

In this classic dish, I reduce the fat by rendering and cooking the bacon slightly before adding it to the main ingredients.

4 ounces lean bacon, diced
2 tablespoons extra-virgin olive oil
1 small onion, chopped
1 16-ounce can plum tomatoes with their juice, chopped
⅛ teaspoon crushed red pepper flakes
1 pound linguine
Freshly ground black pepper to taste
Salt to taste (optional)
Grated Romano cheese
¼ teaspoon crushed red pepper flakes (optional)
Sprigs of fresh basil, for garnish

Serves 4 as a main course or 6 as an appetizer

In a medium skillet, cook the bacon over medium heat until the fat is rendered. Remove the bacon with a slotted spoon, discard the fat, and wipe out the skillet with paper towels.

Heat the olive oil in the skillet, add the onion and bacon, and sauté until the onion is limp. Add the tomatoes and red pepper flakes and simmer for 18 minutes.

While the sauce is simmering, begin cooking the linguine in the usual way (see page 47). When the linguine is nearly done, measure out ¾ cup of the cooking water and add it to the sauce.

Stir the pepper and salt into the sauce and serve over the linguine. Sprinkle with cheese and red pepper flakes and garnish with basil sprigs.

Note: To retain its crispness, fully cooked bacon can be set aside and added to the finished plate of sauced pasta.

THIN SPAGHETTI WITH GARLIC AND OIL

Vermicelli Aglio e Olio

Here's a dish easily prepared with ingredients right off the pantry shelf. I prefer to use the extra-virgin olive oil with its rich bouquet, but some people like a lighter taste. Do try the crushed red pepper flakes for a nice zip.

1 pound thin spaghetti
1 cup extra-virgin olive oil
3 to 4 cloves garlic
½ cup chopped fresh Italian parsley
Freshly grated black pepper to taste
Salt to taste (optional)
¼ teaspoon crushed red pepper flakes (optional)

Serves 4 as a main course or 6 to 8 as an appetizer

Begin cooking the pasta in the usual way (see page 47).

Heat the oil in a medium skillet, sauté the garlic until golden, and discard. Add the parsley, pepper, salt, and red pepper flakes.

Drain the pasta and immediately toss with this sauce.

Pasta alla Carbonara

For whatever reason, I've never been a big fan of spaghetti. I find it too thick, unruly, and ordinary—so instead of Spaghetti Carbonara, here's Pasta alla Carbonara.

I prefer linguine or spaghettini with this sauce, which adheres better to long, thin pasta than to tubular macaroni. If you can find Italian pancetta at a specialty store, by all means use it. If not, substitute lean bacon.

12 ounces spaghettini or linguine
5 ounces *pancetta*, cut into small pieces
1 tablespoon extra-virgin olive oil
2 jumbo eggs, coddled
4 ounces grated Romano cheese
Freshly ground black pepper to taste
2 tablespoons unsalted butter

Serves 4 to 6 as an appetizer or 2 to 3 as a main course

Begin cooking the pasta as usual (see page 47).

Meanwhile, in a large skillet, sauté the *pancetta* in the olive oil until crisp. Remove with a slotted spoon and set aside. Discard all but 2 tablespoons of the oil in the skillet; set aside.

In a bowl, combine the eggs, cheese, and pepper and mix well.

Set aside 2 tablespoons of the pasta cooking water, then drain the pasta. Quickly toss the pasta with the butter, then add the egg mixture and toss.

Transfer the pasta to the skillet with the reserved oil and quickly sauté it until the egg mixture has adhered, adding the pasta water. Sprinkle the reserved *pancetta* over the finished pasta. Serve immediately.

Uncle Tony's Baked Pasta Cake

Pasta al Forno dello Zio Antonio

Uncle Tony, the next to the youngest of Dad's four brothers, was still living at home with my grandmother when I was growing up. Since Gram lived around the corner from us, I was over there every day, eating . . . doing errands for her . . . eating . . . playing . . . eating.

Uncle Tony was a good eater, even though his weight did not show that fact. He loved to make this dish and would eat it hot from the oven or as a cold leftover anytime of the day. I hope you will enjoy Uncle Tony's Baked Pasta Cake as much as he still does.

1 pound spaghetti cooked and well drained
1 tablespoon olive oil
6 large eggs or 10 large egg whites, lightly beaten
1 small onion, chopped
½ cup grated Parmesan cheese
8 ounces pepperoni, chopped
½ teaspoon white pepper
½ cup chopped fresh Italian parsley
Salt to taste (optional)

Serves 6 to 8

Preheat the oven to 350°F. Oil a square baking dish.

In a large bowl, combine the cooked spaghetti, olive oil, beaten eggs or egg whites, chopped onion, Parmesan cheese, pepperoni, white pepper, parsley, and salt. Mix thoroughly. Pour into the dish and bake 45 to 50 minutes or until lightly brown on top.

Pasta with Marinara Sauce

Pasta alla Marinara

You can double this recipe and freeze the leftovers for another time. If you wish to add meat the recipe follows. Serve with your favorite pasta.

1 small onion, chopped
2 cloves garlic
¼ cup olive oil
1 35-ounce can Italian plum tomatoes with their juice
1 teaspoon salt
2 pinches dried basil
1 pinch dried thyme
Freshly ground black pepper to taste
3 ounces tomato paste (optional)
3 ounces water (optional)
1 pound pasta of your choice

Serves 4

In a large skillet, sauté the onion and garlic in the oil for about 5 minutes. Chop the tomatoes coarsely and add with their juices to the skillet. Add the salt, basil, thyme, and pepper. Cook, covered, for 10 minutes; stir and cook, uncovered, for another 20 to 25 minutes.

If you like a thicker sauce, add the tomato paste and water with the tomatoes. While the sauce is simmering, begin cooking the pasta. When ready, serve sauce over the pasta.

PASTA WITH TOMATO MEAT SAUCE

Pasta al Sugo di Carne

Here again you can double this recipe and freeze the leftovers for another time. Serve it with your favorite pasta.

1 recipe meatballs (page 163)
1 pound lean round steak, ground
6 Italian sausages
¼ cup olive oil
1 small onion, chopped
2 cloves garlic
1 35-ounce can Italian plum tomatoes with their juice
3 ounces tomato paste
3 ounces water
1 teaspoon salt
2 pinches dried basil
1 pinch dried thyme
Freshly ground black pepper to taste
1 pound pasta of your choice

Serves 4 to 6

In a large skillet, sauté the meatballs, ground beef, and sausages briefly in a little of the olive oil; drain off the fat.

Meanwhile, in another skillet, sauté the onion and garlic in the remaining oil for about 5 minutes. Chop the tomatoes coarsely, and add with their juices to the skillet. Add the tomato paste, water, salt, basil, thyme, and pepper and simmer, covered, for 30 minutes.

Add the meat to the sauce and cook, covered, an additional 30 minutes. Remove the cover, stir, and cook another 20 to 25 minutes.

While the sauce is simmering begin cooking the pasta. When ready, serve sauce over the pasta.

LASAGNE

When I was growing up, one of my favorite dishes was lasagne. Oh, so good. And when you look at all the ingredients, you can see that it is also a powerhouse of nutrition, delivering several offerings from the food pyramid. You can cut down on the fat by using low-fat cheese and skipping the meat in the sauce.

Many people prefer lasagne when it's a day old, claiming it has even better flavor. Yes, you can freeze lasagne, so make plenty.

1 pound lasagne
1 pound ricotta cheese (part-skim or low-fat)
1 whole egg, beaten
2 egg whites, beaten
½ cup grated Parmesan cheese
½ cup chopped fresh Italian parsley
¼ teaspoon grated nutmeg
¼ teaspoon dried basil
Freshly ground black pepper to taste
Salt to taste (optional)
1 recipe tomato meat sauce (page 68)
8 ounces mozzarella cheese (part-skim or low-fat), shredded

Serves 6 to 8 as a main course

Cook the pasta in boiling water until *al dente*. Drain, rinse in cold water, and drain again.

In large bowl, mix together the ricotta, eggs, Parmesan cheese, parsley, nutmeg, basil, pepper, and salt.

Preheat the oven to 350°F. Oil a rectangular baking dish approximately 13" × 9" × 2" and spoon some sauce into the bottom. Make a layer of pasta on the bottom, spread some ricotta mixture on top, and sprinkle with mozzarella. Ladle on some of the sauce. Repeat with the layers of pasta, ricotta, mozzarella, and sauce until all the ingredients except the sauce are used up, ending with pasta on top with a coating of sauce. Cover and bake for approximately 40 minutes. Let stand before serving. Serve with a little extra sauce.

Florentine Lasagne

Lasagne alla Fiorentina

A change of pace from the original, with the Florentine touch of spinach.

1 recipe Lasagne (page 69)
1 10-ounce package frozen chopped spinach, thawed, no need to cook,
  drained, and squeezed dry

Serves 6 to 8 as a main course

Incorporate the spinach into the ricotta mixture and proceed as directed.

Manicotti

Making manicotti today is not the labor-intensive chore it was when Mom made it, thanks to ready-formed dried pasta tubes. There are even "no-boil" boxed pasta sheets that you soak in water, then use as cooked pasta. Just cut, fill, and roll up.

8 large pasta tubes
1 pound ricotta (part-skim, low-fat, or no-fat)
½ cup grated Parmesan cheese, plus extra for serving
2 tablespoons chopped fresh Italian parsley
¼ teaspoon grated nutmeg
1 teaspoon dried basil
Freshly grated pepper to taste
Salt to taste (optional)
1 recipe marinara sauce (page 67)

Serves 4 to 6

Preheat the oven to 350°F. Cook the pasta as usual (see page 47). Drain, rinse in cold water, and drain well again.

Meanwhile, in a large bowl, combine the ricotta, Parmesan cheese, parsley, nutmeg, basil, pepper, and salt and mix well.

Oil a medium baking dish and spoon some of the tomato sauce into the bottom. Fill the manicotti shells (tubes) with the cheese mixture, then ladle the sauce on top of each shell. Bake, uncovered, for 20 minutes, or until bubbling.

Sprinkle grated cheese on top and serve.

CANNELLONI

Cannelloni is similar to manicotti, but the filling is a combination of meat and vegetables. The food processor makes an especially smooth filling.

12 large pasta tubes
1 tablespoon olive oil
1 tablespoon unsalted butter
1 small onion, chopped
1 slice prosciutto, or ham, chopped
1 cup chicken broth (recipe on page 15)
1 large chicken breast (1½-pound), skinned and boned
½ cup chopped mushrooms
½ cup white wine
2 large egg whites
¼ teaspoon grated nutmeg
¼ teaspoon white pepper
Salt to taste (optional)
¼ cup grated Parmesan cheese
1 tablespoon chopped fresh Italian parsley
2 tablespoons bread crumbs
1 recipe marinara sauce (page 67)

Serves 6

(continued)

Cook the pasta in the usual way until *al dente* (see page 47). Drain, rinse in cold water, and drain again.

Heat the oil and butter in a large skillet. Add the onion and sauté briefly. When soft, add the prosciutto, chicken broth, chicken, mushrooms, and white wine. Cover and simmer approximately 12 to 15 minutes, until the chicken is cooked and the liquid is reduced.

Preheat the oven to 375°F. Transfer the skillet mixture to a food processor and process into a fine paste. Transfer to a bowl, add the egg whites, nutmeg, pepper, salt, Parmesan cheese, parsley, and bread crumbs, and mix well.

Oil a baking dish and spoon some of the tomato sauce on the bottom. Fill the pasta tubes with meat and vegetable mixture and ladle sauce on top of each tube. Bake, uncovered, for about 20 minutes.

POLENTA

There are times in every household when a mother hears the cry "What is there to eat?" When my brother and I let forth with this cry, Mom would fix polenta. Sometimes she'd make it with just butter and grated cheese, but we'd be doubly pleased when she ladled tomato sauce on top. Today, when I serve my Italian soul food to guests, I swirl designs with the sauce to fancy it up. Here is the way my mother made it.

1 tablespoon olive oil
Salt to taste (optional)
4 cups water
1 cup yellow cornmeal

Serves 4 to 6

In a large pot, mix the olive oil, salt, and water and bring to a boil. Sprinkle in the cornmeal, shaking it through a large sieve to prevent lumps from forming. Simmer, uncovered, stirring constantly.

When all of the water is absorbed and the mixture is of medium-thick consistency—about 6 to 8 minutes—the polenta is ready to serve.

POLENTA WITH SAUCE
Polenta al Sugo

1 recipe Polenta (page 72)
1 cup or more marinara sauce (recipe on page 67)
Grated Parmesan cheese
Freshly ground black pepper to taste

Serves 4 to 6

Ladle the polenta into bowls, make a shallow well in the center, then fill with the sauce. Pass around extra sauce, the cheese, and the pepper mill.

FRIED POLENTA
Polenta Fritta

1 recipe Polenta (page 72)
Oil for frying

Serves 4 to 6

Pour the hot polenta into a large rectangular baking dish. Spread out to an inch thick. Refrigerate.

When firm, cut into 3- by 2-inch pieces and fry until golden on each side.

GRILLED POLENTA
Polenta alla Griglia

Same as the preceding recipe, except the polenta is done on the grill. Use a barbecue screen to prevent the slices from slipping through the grates.

BAKED POLENTA WITH RICOTTA CHEESE AND SAUSAGES

Polenta Pasticciata con Ricotta e Salsiccia

This casserole is a perfect example of combining spicy sausage and satiny ricotta cheese. Great for a Sunday TV football brunch.

1 teaspoon olive oil
1 recipe Polenta (page 72)
1 pound sweet Italian sausages, casings removed and crumbled
1 15-ounce container ricotta cheese (low-fat or no-fat)
2 tablespoons grated Parmesan cheese
¼ teaspoon dried thyme
Salt to taste (optional)
Freshly ground black pepper to taste

Serves 4 to 6

Preheat the oven to 375°F. Grease an 8½-inch square baking dish with the olive oil. Pour in the polenta and spread it to an inch in thickness. Set aside. In a medium skillet, sauté the sausage until browned.

Spread the ricotta cheese over the polenta, followed by the sausage, then sprinkle with the Parmesan cheese, thyme, salt, and pepper. Bake about 30 minutes.

CHAPTER 5

❧

Vegetables
Verdure e Cortorni

At my mother's table, as in any good Italian home, vegetables were given their own star status. They were carried forth on heaping platters and then portioned onto special individual plates. They were never, never demoted to color accents for the meat or fish dishes.

Often there was golden zucchini, sautéed with fennel seeds in a little olive oil, piles of string beans touched with lemon juice and flecks of pine nuts, roasted peppers charred black for flavor, stuffed artichokes, stuffed potatoes, and potato croquettes.

When Mom cooked a pork roast meal, she always made little white onions with sweet and sour sauce that were so rich tasting, my brother and I never realized we were eating vegetables.

But my all-time favorite was always the pick of Dad's backyard tomato crop. We had tomatoes many different ways, but the most memorable is a toss-up between Grandma's baked tomato treat and freshly sliced tomatoes simply dressed with a bit of basil and olive oil.

STUFFED ARTICHOKES

Carciofi Ripieni

There have been times when I would sit at the kitchen table eating Mom's stuffed artichokes and with each leaf I would say to myself, as with my first loves, "She loves me! She loves me not!"

One of the oldest foods known to man, artichokes were first cultivated in the Mediterranean basin and are now grown in California. Stir-fried, steamed alone, or cooked with other ingredients, they are as healthy as they are tasty!

Here's the traditional Italian stuffed artichoke. Some aficionados never cover artichokes when cooking for fear they will become bitter. You be the judge.

6 large artichokes
Juice of ½ lemon, for soaking
2 cloves garlic
1 small onion, minced
½ to ⅔ cup olive oil
1½ cups Italian-seasoned bread crumbs
1 tablespoon fresh lemon juice
¼ cup grated Parmesan cheese
2 tablespoons minced fresh Italian parsley
Freshly ground black pepper to taste
Salt to taste (optional)

Serves 6

Cut off the stems and the top fourth of the artichokes. Trim off the prickly points of the leaves with scissors. Turn the artichokes upside down and gently press down to loosen the leaves. Open the leaves and let the artichokes soak in a large bowl of water with juice of ½ lemon.

In a small skillet, quickly sauté the garlic and onion in the olive oil until just tender. Add the bread crumbs, lemon juice, Parmesan cheese, parsley, pepper and salt. Remove from the heat.

Drain the artichokes and stuff the mixture between the leaves.

Place the artichokes in a pan large enough to hold them side by side upright. Add enough water to come ⅓ up the sides of the artichokes. Cover and bring the water to a simmer over low heat. Simmer for approximately 30 minutes. Allow one whole artichoke per serving.

ASPARAGUS MILANESE
Asparagi alla Milanese

Asparagus was prized by the ancient Romans (including one or two in my family) for its medicinal value (significant vitamin C, good potassium, excellent folic acid, plus fiber) as well as its wonderful taste.

Choose thick or thin stalks, according to your preference. By the way, I do not peel asparagus but just cut or break off the woody, pulpy ends.

1½ pounds asparagus
1 tablespoon unsalted butter
2 tablespoons olive oil
3 tablespoons grated Parmesan cheese
Salt to taste (optional)
Freshly ground black pepper to taste

Serves 4 to 6

Steam the asparagus in a covered stockpot large enough to accommodate the stems. Meanwhile, in a large skillet, melt the butter in the oil. Add the almost-cooked asparagus to the skillet and sauté for a few minutes. Sprinkle with Parmesan cheese, salt, and pepper.

Sautéed Broccoli with Garlic

Broccoli in Padella

1 head fresh broccoli (or 2 10-ounce packages frozen broccoli spears)
2 cloves garlic
3 tablespoons olive oil
1 tablespoon fresh lemon juice
Freshly ground black pepper to taste
Salt to taste (optional)

Serves 4 to 6

Steam the broccoli in a large covered saucepan. Meanwhile, in a large skillet, sauté the garlic in the oil, then add the lemon juice. When the broccoli is almost cooked, add it to the skillet and sauté for a few minutes, or until cooked to your taste. Season with pepper and salt.

Broccoli Parmesan

Broccoli alla Parmigiana

Many people think that "alla parmigiana" means hidden under a thick blanket of cheese. But in Italian households, parmigiana refers to the dusting of good quality cheese used in the recipe.

1 head fresh broccoli (or 2 10-ounce packages frozen broccoli spears)
2 cloves garlic, crushed
2 tablespoons unsalted butter
2 tablespoons olive oil
¼ cup grated Parmesan cheese
Salt to taste (optional)
Freshly ground black pepper to taste

Serves 4 to 6

Preheat the oven to 350°F. Steam the broccoli in a large covered saucepan until crisp-tender.

Meanwhile, sauté the garlic in the butter and oil and discard when golden. Place the broccoli in a baking dish, drizzle the butter and oil over it, and sprinkle with Parmesan cheese, salt, and pepper. Bake for approximately 20 minutes.

ROASTED GARLIC
Aglio Arrosto

We usually think of garlic as a flavoring, an herb, and an integral part of many Italian dishes. I'd like to introduce garlic "The Side Dish"! Delicious served with roasted meats. The soft roasted garlic purée is wonderful on bread with a little olive oil in place of butter.

6 large whole heads garlic
Olive oil
Rosemary

Serves 6

Preheat the oven to 325°F. Liberally brush the garlic with olive oil and sprinkle some rosemary on each. Or top with fresh rosemary sprigs dipped in oil. Cover loosely with aluminum foil.

Place in a small baking dish and bake for 1¾ hours.

Brussels Sprouts Vinaigrette
Cavolini di Bruxel

Even those who claim to loathe Brussels sprouts will be tempted to try these. Substitute bottled dressing if you must.

1 pint fresh Brussels sprouts (or 1 10-ounce package frozen Brussels sprouts), cut into quarters if large, cut into halves if small
2 tablespoons Balsamic Vinaigrette (recipe on page 40)
2 tablespoons water
2 tablespoons sliced almonds or pine nuts
½ teaspoon white pepper
Salt to taste (optional)

Serves 4

In a medium covered saucepan, steam the Brussels sprouts in the vinaigrette dressing and water until tender. Add the sliced almonds or pine nuts, pepper, and salt. Toss and serve.

Fried Eggplant
Melanzane Fritte

1 medium eggplant, peeled
2 tablespoons grated Parmesan cheese
1 cup fine bread crumbs
½ teaspoon oregano
Salt to taste (optional)
Freshly ground black pepper to taste
2 large eggs, beaten
Oil for frying

Serves 4 to 6

Slice the eggplant about ½ inch thick, sprinkle with salt, and place in a colander to drain for 30 minutes. Pat dry with paper towels and cut into finger-length strips.

In a shallow dish, combine the Parmesan cheese, bread crumbs, oregano, salt, and pepper. Dip the eggplant strips into the egg, then coat with the bread crumb mixture.

Heat oil in a large deep-fryer or skillet. Fry the eggplant in small batches. Drain on paper towels to remove excess oil. Serve hot.

EGGPLANT WITH PROSCIUTTO AND PARMESAN CHEESE

Melanzane alla Parmigiana con Prosciutto

1 medium eggplant, peeled
Oil for frying
2 cups marinara sauce (recipe on page 67)
3 ounces prosciutto, thinly sliced
⅓ cup grated Parmesan cheese
1 cup shredded mozzarella cheese
Freshly ground black pepper to taste
Salt to taste (optional)

Serves 4 to 6

Slice the eggplant crosswise ½ inch thick. Salt the slices and place in colander to drain for 30 minutes. Remove and pat dry.

Preheat the oven to 375°F. Heat oil in a large skillet and fry the eggplant slices until golden. Drain on paper towels.

Pour a small amount of the tomato sauce on the bottom of a 12- by 7-inch baking dish. Layer with eggplant slices. Top with prosciutto and sprinkle with some Parmesan cheese. Add another layer of eggplant, then sprinkle with the rest of the Parmesan. Top with the mozzarella cheese and drizzle on the sauce, pepper and salt.

Bake, uncovered, for about 30 minutes.

STUFFED EGGPLANT

Melanzane Ripiene

Try this as a main course, and use white eggplant if it's available.

1 medium eggplant, peeled
Olive oil for frying
1 small onion, minced
1 tablespoon drained small capers
2 tablespoons chopped fresh Italian parsley
¼ teaspoon dried oregano
¼ teaspoon dried basil
1 cup part-skim ricotta cheese
¼ cup grated Romano cheese
Freshly ground black pepper to taste
Salt to taste (optional)
2 cups marinara sauce (recipe on page 67)

Serves 4 to 6

Slice the eggplant lengthwise about ¼ inch thick. Place in a colander, sprinkle with salt, and let stand in the sink for about 45 minutes to purge it of bitter juices. Remove and pat the slices dry.

Preheat the oven to 375°F. In a large skillet, fry the eggplant slices in the olive oil on both sides until tender but not mushy. Remove and drain on paper towels.

In the same skillet, sauté the onion, capers, parsley, oregano, and basil. When the onion is soft, transfer the mixture to a large bowl. Mix with the ricotta cheese, Romano cheese, pepper, and salt.

Place about 1 tablespoon of the cheese mixture on each slice of eggplant and roll lengthwise. Place in a baking dish, seam side down, and bake for about 30 minutes.

Remove from the oven and top with marinara sauce before serving.

SAUTÉED CAULIFLOWER
Cavolfiore in Padella

1 head fresh cauliflower (or 2 10-ounce packages frozen cauliflower
  florets)
2 cloves garlic, crushed
1 tablespoon unsalted butter
2 tablespoons olive oil
3 tablespoons grated Parmesan cheese
Salt to taste (optional)
Freshly ground black pepper to taste

Serves 4 to 6

Steam the cauliflower in a large covered saucepan. Meanwhile, in a large
skillet, sauté the garlic in the butter and oil and discard when golden. Add
the almost-cooked cauliflower to the skillet and sauté for a few minutes.
　Sprinkle with Parmesan cheese and add salt and pepper.

CAULIFLOWER CROQUETTES
Crocchette di Cavolfiore

1 head fresh cauliflower (or 2 10-ounce packages frozen cauliflower
  florets)
2 large eggs or 4 large egg whites, beaten
2 ounces grated Parmesan cheese
2 tablespoons chopped fresh Italian parsley
Pinch grated nutmeg
½ teaspoon white pepper
Salt to taste (optional)
½ cup grated Mozzarella cheese (optional)
1 cup bread crumbs
Olive oil for frying

Serves 6 to 8

(continued)

In a large covered saucepan, steam the cauliflower until tender, then mash. Add the eggs, Parmesan cheese, parsley, nutmeg, pepper, salt, and mozzarella if desired.

Mix together and form into patties about 3 inches across. Coat with bread crumbs and refrigerate an hour or more to firm up.

In a large skillet, fry the croquettes in olive oil until golden brown.

CARAMELIZED ONIONS

Cipolle Caramellate

This is perhaps the onion at its finest. Great with roasts, steaks, or poultry.

6 medium to large onions
2 tablespoons olive oil
3 tablespoons brown sugar

Serves 6

Preheat the oven to 375°F. Brush the onions with the olive oil. Scoop out a small well (1 inch deep) on top of each onion; fill with brown sugar.

Place side by side in shallow baking dish and bake for 1½ to 2 hours.

ONIONS AND PEAS

Cipolline e Piselli

12 ounces fresh pearl onions (or 1 10-ounce package frozen pearl
  onions)
¾ cup chicken broth (recipe on page 15)
¼ teaspoon grated nutmeg
2 tablespoons unsalted butter
12 ounces shelled fresh peas (or 1 10-ounce package frozen peas)
Freshly ground black pepper to taste
Salt to taste (optional)

Serves 6 to 8

Place the onions and broth in a large saucepan, add the nutmeg, cover, and
bring to a boil. Then reduce the heat to a simmer and cook until the broth
has almost evaporated and the onions are soft. Add the butter, peas, pepper,
and salt. Continue to cook, covered, until the peas are tender.

KIDNEY BEANS AND ONIONS
Fagioli e Cipolle

An unlikely combination that works well. The brown sugar adds just the right touch of sweetness.

2 medium onions, chopped
1 stalk celery, chopped
2 tablespoons olive oil
1 15 to 18-ounce can kidney beans, undrained
2 tablespoons tomato paste
½ cup chicken broth (recipe on page 15)
1 teaspoon brown sugar
½ teaspoon white pepper
1 teaspoon dried oregano
1 tablespoon fresh lemon juice
Salt to taste (optional)

Serves 4 to 6

In a large skillet, sauté the onions and celery in the olive oil until the onions are translucent. Add the beans and stir in the tomato paste and broth. Add the brown sugar, pepper, oregano, lemon juice, and salt and simmer for 15 minutes.

SWEET AND SOUR WHITE ONIONS
Cipolline All'Agrodolce

Capers are the buds of a shrub from the Mediterranean. Their pungent flavor is combined with the vinegar and sugar to give these onions a sweet and sour flavor that complements pork roast or other hearty meats.

1½ pounds pearl onions
1 tablespoon unsalted butter
3 tablespoons olive oil
2 tablespoons drained capers, rinsed
2 tablespoons brown sugar
3 tablespoons white vinegar
½ teaspoon white pepper
Salt to taste (optional)

Serves 4 to 6

Steam the onions in a large covered saucepan. Meanwhile, in a large skillet, melt the butter in the oil. Add the almost-cooked onions to the skillet and sauté, turning frequently, for several minutes.

Add the capers, stir in the sugar, then add the vinegar, pepper, and salt. Cook for an additional 2 to 4 minutes. The sauce should coat the onions.

"VEGE MELT"

Pasta al Formaggio Pepperoni

The Love Chef's quick, Italian-style macaroni and cheese.

2 cloves garlic
2 ounces extra-virgin olive oil
1 red bell pepper, cut into thin strips
1 medium red onion, sliced
1 tablespoon hot pepper sauce
1 cup cooked *acini di pepe* or other small pasta
1 cup shredded low-fat cheese of your choice
Freshly ground black pepper to taste

Serves 4

Sauté the garlic in the oil, then add the bell pepper and onion. When the onion is translucent, add the hot pepper sauce, pasta, and cheese and pepper. Toss quickly to heat through. Serve immediately.

SAUTÉED SPINACH
Spinaci in Padella

I love this dish for the heavenly perfume of the garlic and the glisten of good-quality olive oil. It may sound heretical, but often frozen spinach is a better choice than the limp, tasteless, and sandy stuff found in many markets during the off-season—and you don't have to worry about rinsing off all the sand.

2 pounds fresh spinach (or 2 10-ounce packages frozen spinach)
2 cloves garlic
2 tablespoons olive oil
1 tablespoon unsalted butter
¼ teaspoon grated nutmeg
Salt to taste (optional)
Freshly ground black pepper to taste

Serves 4 to 6

Steam the spinach in a large covered saucepan. Meanwhile, in a large skillet, sauté the garlic in the olive oil and butter. Add the almost-cooked spinach, to the skillet, then the nutmeg, salt, and pepper, and sauté for a few minutes.

SPINACH WITH ANCHOVY SAUCE

Spinaci alle Acciughe

One of my favorites! The combination of spinach and anchovies betrays this dish's Piedmontese origins. Wonderful served along with fish.

1½ pounds fresh spinach (or 2 10-ounce packages frozen spinach, thawed)
2 cloves garlic
1 tablespoon unsalted butter
2 tablespoons olive oil
3 anchovy fillets, rinsed
Salt to taste (optional)
Freshly ground black pepper to taste

Serves 4 to 6

Steam the spinach for 4 to 5 minutes in a large covered saucepan. Meanwhile, in a large skillet, sauté the garlic in the butter and oil. Add the anchovies and stir until they blend into the oil-butter mixture to make a sauce. Add salt and pepper.

Drain the spinach, add to the skillet, and stir-fry until well coated with the sauce.

ZUCCHINI WITH OIL AND LEMON

Zucchini all'Agro

Lemon adds a quick zest to any recipe, but when it is combined with olive oil it's ambrosia.

4–6 small to medium zucchini
2 cloves garlic
3 tablespoons olive oil
1 tablespoon fresh lemon juice
1 teaspoon fennel seeds
Salt to taste (optional)
Freshly ground black pepper to taste

Serves 4 to 6

Steam the zucchini whole in a large covered saucepan for 6 to 8 minutes. Meanwhile, in a large skillet, sauté the garlic in the oil until golden, then discard. Add the lemon juice to the skillet.

When the zucchini are almost cooked, remove them from the saucepan and slice. Sauté the slices in the lemon-oil mixture until golden. Sprinkle with fennel seeds, salt, and pepper.

ZUCCHINI-TOMATO CASSEROLE

Zucchini e Pomodori

6 medium zucchini
2 cloves garlic, crushed
1 red onion, thinly sliced
2 tablespoons olive oil
6 very ripe plum tomatoes, sliced
½ cup grated Parmesan cheese
3 tablespoons chopped fresh Italian parsley
1 teaspoon dried oregano
Salt to taste (optional)
¼ teaspoon crushed red pepper flakes
Freshly ground black pepper to taste

Serves 6 to 8

Preheat the oven to 350°F. Cut the zucchini in half, then thinly slice each half lengthwise.

In a medium skillet, sauté the garlic and onion in the olive oil until the onion is translucent.

Oil a baking dish and cover the bottom with zucchini slices, then tomato slices, half of the Parmesan cheese, and half of the parsley, oregano, salt, and red pepper flakes. Scatter half of the onion and repeat the process until all the ingredients are used. Top off with freshly grated pepper.

Bake for 40 to 45 minutes.

TURNIP GREENS

Rape

Turnip greens are bitter and therefore an acquired taste. They're great with beans, pork, lamb, and game.

2 pounds turnip greens
½ cup water
2 cloves garlic, crushed
3 tablespoons olive oil
1 tablespoon fresh lemon juice
Salt to taste (optional)
Freshly ground black pepper to taste
1 lemon, cut into wedges

Serves 4 to 6

Clean the greens, discarding any heavy stalks, then chop. Steam the greens in the water in a large covered saucepan.

Meanwhile, in a large skillet, sauté the garlic in the olive oil, then add the lemon juice. When the greens are almost cooked, add them to the skillet and sauté for a few minutes, or until cooked to your taste. Season with salt and pepper and serve with lemon wedges.

SAUTÉED ESCAROLE

Scarola in Padella

Escarole loses most of its characteristic bitterness when sautéed with fennel seeds and lemon juice. This dish is lovely with pork or chicken.

1 large head escarole, chopped
1 teaspoon fennel seeds
2 cloves garlic
1 tablespoon unsalted butter
2 tablespoons olive oil
Juice of ½ lemon
Salt to taste (optional)
Freshly ground black pepper to taste

Serves 4 to 6

In a large covered saucepan, steam the escarole with the fennel seeds until barely tender. Drain and set aside. Meanwhile, in a large skillet, briefly sauté the garlic in the butter and oil. Add the escarole, lemon juice, salt, and pepper and sauté for a few minutes more, until heated through.

SAUTÉED SWISS CHARD

Bietola in Padella

1½ pounds Swiss chard
½ cup water
2 cloves garlic
3 tablespoons olive oil
2 tablespoons lemon juice
Salt to taste (optional)
Freshly ground black pepper to taste

Serves 4 to 6

Thoroughly clean the Swiss chard. The ribs of the larger stems may be peeled. Cut up the stems and leaves and steam them briefly in the water in a covered saucepan until barely tender.

Meanwhile, in a large skillet, sauté the garlic in the olive oil. Add the steamed Swiss chard and lemon juice to the skillet and sauté for a few minutes. Add the salt and pepper.

SAUTÉED RADICCHIO

Radicchio in Padella

This recipe serves as proof that the handsome radicchio leaf is more than just garnish. Also known as red chicory, the leaf is delicious sautéed with a touch of balsamic vinegar.

2 cloves garlic, crushed
2 tablespoons extra-virgin olive oil
12 ounces radicchio, whole leaves
2 tablespoons balsamic vinegar
Freshly ground black pepper to taste
Salt to taste (optional)

Serves 4 to 6

In a large skillet, sauté the garlic in the oil. Add the radicchio and quickly sauté until wilted. Add the vinegar, pepper, and salt and serve immediately.

SAUTÉED STRING BEANS
Fagiolini in Padella

2 cloves garlic
3 tablespoons olive oil
1 pound fresh string beans (or 2 10-ounce packages frozen green beans)
1 tablespoon fresh lemon juice
Salt to taste (optional)
Freshly ground black pepper to taste
2 tablespoons pine nuts, toasted (optional)

Serves 4 to 6

In a large skillet, sauté the garlic in the olive oil. Add the string beans, lemon juice, salt, and pepper and continue to sauté until cooked to your taste. Toss with pine nuts before serving.

ROASTED PEPPERS
Pepperoni Arrosto

I can't begin to tell you how many times I saw my grandmother and mother put a pepper directly on the stove over a gas jet and blister it until the pepper was black. The broiler method I use here cooks the peppers from the inside out. This method produces a softer pepper that is more easily flavored by the dressing.

2 large red bell peppers
2 large yellow bell peppers
12 green olives, pitted and halved
¼ cup extra virgin olive oil
1 tablespoon fresh lemon juice
1½ teaspoons dried basil
1 stalk celery, sliced very thinly
Freshly ground black pepper to taste
Salt to taste (optional)

Serves 4 to 6

On a baking sheet, roast the peppers close to the broiler flame or heat. Use tongs to turn them so they blister evenly. When the peppers are fully charred (yes, *black*), remove them and put them in a clean paper bag. Shake off the charring by rubbing the peppers against each other. Remove the peppers when cool and peel away any remaining skin.

Quarter the peppers and discard the seeds. Arrange on a plate with the olives.

In a small bowl, combine the olive oil, lemon juice, basil, celery, black pepper, and salt; let stand for several minutes, then drizzle over the peppers and olives. Let stand for several minutes (or refrigerate) before serving.

SAUTÉED FAVA BEANS
Fave in Padella

Fava beans can be found fresh in some green markets. The taste is worth the effort in locating them, especially when you combine them with prosciutto. This recipe is literally the Italian version of pork and beans!

2 ounces prosciutto ham, diced
1 small onion, minced
2 tablespoons olive oil
1 pound shelled fava beans
½ cup chicken broth (recipe on page 15)
Salt to taste (optional)
Freshly ground black pepper to taste

Serves 4 to 6

In a medium skillet, sauté the prosciutto and onion in the olive oil. When the onion is translucent, add the beans, broth, salt, and pepper. Cover and cook for 25 to 30 minutes, stirring occasionally.

Mushrooms with Anchovy-Mint Sauce

Funghi alle Acciughe

In this Roman dish, mint replaces basil in the place of prominence. It works well with the anchovies to produce an unusual and delicious sauce.

2 cloves garlic
¼ cup olive oil
2 anchovy fillets
4 plum tomatoes, chopped
2 sprigs mint, chopped
Salt to taste (optional)
Freshly ground black pepper to taste
1 pound mushrooms, sliced

Serves 4 to 6

In a medium skillet, sauté the garlic in the oil and discard when golden. Add the anchovies to the skillet and stir until they blend into the oil. Then add the tomatoes, mint, salt, and pepper and cook, covered, for 5 minutes. Add the mushrooms and cook for an additional 10 minutes.

CRABMEAT-STUFFED MUSHROOMS

Funghi Ripieni

12 to 18 medium mushrooms
1 cup fresh crabmeat, removed from the shell and broken apart
  (or 1 6½-ounce can crabmeat)
3 tablespoons unsalted butter, melted
¼ cup cracker meal
2 tablespoons mayonnaise
¼ teaspoon white pepper
1 tablespoon dry white vermouth
1 tablespoon grated Parmesan cheese
Salt to taste (optional)
1 to 2 cups milk
Chopped fresh Italian parsley, for garnish

Serves 6 to 8

Preheat the oven to 300°F. Remove the stems from the mushroom caps and discard. Wipe the caps with a damp sponge or paper towel and set aside.

Pick over the crabmeat to remove any cartilage. Place in a bowl and mix in the butter, cracker meal, mayonnaise, pepper, vermouth, grated Parmesan, and salt. Stuff each mushroom cap with spoonfuls of the mixture, mounding it high in the center. (Any leftover filling can be frozen and used another time.)

Place the caps in a small baking dish or pan just large enough to accommodate them snugly, and pour in the milk, which should come to the top of the mushrooms, just below the stuffing.

Bake until tender, approximately 45 minutes. Remove to a serving dish with a slotted spoon and decorate with parsley.

Baked Tomatoes

Pomodori al Forno

4 to 6 medium ripe tomatoes
1 tablespoon chopped fresh basil
2 cloves garlic, minced
3 tablespoons extra-virgin olive oil
½ teaspoon dried oregano
¾ cup bread crumbs
1 tablespoon grated Parmesan cheese
Freshly ground black pepper to taste
Salt to taste (optional)

Serves 4 to 6

Preheat the oven to 375°F. Slice off the tops of the tomatoes and scoop out about ½ inch of the centers.

In a small bowl, mix the basil, garlic, olive oil, oregano, bread crumbs, cheese, pepper, and salt. Spoon the mixture onto the tomatoes and bake until the crumbs are browned, about 15 minutes.

Tomato and Basil Pie

Torta di Pomodori e Basilico

1 9-inch pie shell
3 medium tomatoes, sliced, then cut in half
¼ cup chopped scallion, including green
¾ cup chopped prosciutto
2 tablespoons chopped fresh basil
¼ teaspoon dried oregano
Freshly ground black pepper to taste
1 cup grated provolone cheese
¼ cup mayonnaise
⅛ teaspoon grated nutmeg

Serves 6

Cooking with Love, Italian Style

Preheat the oven to 450°F. Bake the pie shell for 6 minutes and then remove.

Arrange the tomato slices in the shell. Add the scallion, prosciutto, basil, oregano, and pepper. Combine the cheese, mayonnaise and nutmeg and spread on top, covering the pie entirely. Bake for approximately 35 minutes.

GRANDMA'S BAKED TOMATO TREAT
Pomodori della Nonna

I was asked to come up with several recipes for a "Tomato Mania" segment on Live with Regis and Kathie Lee. *The recipes that follow were big hits!*

1 medium onion, sliced
1 tablespoon unsalted butter
12 slices lightly toasted white bread, crusts removed
2 tablespoons olive oil
3 medium tomatoes, peeled and sliced
10 ounces spinach, cooked and drained well
¼ teaspoon grated nutmeg
1 cup shredded low-fat mozzarella cheese
Freshly ground black pepper to taste

Serves 6

Preheat the oven to 350°F. In a small skillet, sauté the onion in the butter until translucent.

Brush the toast on both sides with the olive oil. Line the bottom and sides of a loaf pan with the toast, cutting to fit.

Layer in half of the tomatoes, then the onion and spinach. Sprinkle with the nutmeg and add the rest of the tomatoes. Top with the cheese and pepper to taste. Bake for approximately 30 minutes.

POTATO CHEESE FRITTATA
Frittata di Patate e Formaggio

You've probably enjoyed quiches and omelettes, but on the next few pages are several frittatas—hearty Italian style—leading off with my favorite. If you're watching your cholesterol, it is possible to use egg substitutes and egg whites, but of course the taste is not quite the same.

3 medium red potatoes, cooked in their skins and thickly sliced
1 red bell pepper, cored, seeded, and diced
1 medium onion, thinly sliced
3 tablespoons olive oil
3 tablespoons unsalted butter
8 large eggs
1 cup shredded low-fat cheese
½ teaspoon dried thyme
Freshly ground black pepper to taste

Serves 4 to 6

In a large skillet, sauté the potatoes, bell pepper, and onion in the olive oil and butter until the onion is translucent.

In a medium bowl, beat the eggs until frothy, then stir in the cheese, thyme, and black pepper. Pour the mixture evenly into the skillet and shake it into place.

When the bottom is formed and browned, put a large heatproof plate over the skillet, flip, then slide the frittata back into the skillet to cook the top. If you do not feel confident enough to do this, put the skillet under the broiler for 3 to 4 minutes (be sure the skillet has a flameproof handle).

ZUCCHINI FRITTATA

Frittata di Zucchini

This recipe summons memories of Saturday lunch at the Anthony household, where I would pile frittata onto fresh Italian bread and top the whole concoction with ketchup—an act of treason in my mother's eyes.

2 to 3 medium zucchini, thinly sliced
1 medium onion, thinly sliced
3 tablespoons olive oil
3 tablespoons unsalted butter
8 large eggs
2 tablespoons grated Parmesan cheese
½ teaspoon dried thyme
Freshly ground black pepper to taste
Salt to taste (optional)

Serves 4 to 6

In a large skillet, sauté the zucchini and onion in the olive oil and butter until the onion is translucent.

In a medium bowl, beat the eggs until frothy, then stir in the cheese, thyme, pepper, and salt. Pour the mixture evenly into the skillet and shake it into place.

When the bottom is formed and browned, put a large heatproof plate over the skillet, flip, then slide the frittata back into the skillet to cook the top. If you do not feel confident enough to do this, put the skillet under the broiler for 3 to 4 minutes (be sure the skillet has a flameproof handle).

Spinach Cheese Frittata

Frittata di Spinaci e Formaggio

½ pound fresh spinach, chopped (or 1 10-ounce package frozen
  chopped spinach)
1 red bell pepper, cored, seeded, and diced
1 medium onion, thinly sliced
3 tablespoons olive oil
3 tablespoons unsalted butter
8 large eggs
1 cup shredded low-fat cheese
½ teaspoon grated nutmeg
½ teaspoon dried thyme
Salt to taste (optional)
Freshly ground black pepper to taste

Serves 4 to 6

In a large skillet, sauté the spinach, bell pepper, and onion in the olive oil and butter until the onion is translucent.

In a medium bowl, beat the eggs until frothy, then stir in the cheese, nutmeg, thyme, salt, and black pepper. Pour the mixture evenly into the skillet and shake it into place.

When the bottom is formed and browned, put a large heatproof plate over the skillet, flip, then slide the frittata back into the skillet to cook the top. If you do not feel confident enough to do this, put the skillet under the broiler for 3 to 4 minutes (be sure the skillet has a flameproof handle).

ZUCCHINI CHEESE FRITTATA

Frittata de Zucchini e Formaggio

2 medium fresh zucchini, diced
1 red bell pepper, cored, seeded, and diced
1 medium onion, thinly sliced
3 tablespoons olive oil
3 tablespoons unsalted butter
8 large eggs
1 cup shredded low-fat cheese
2 tablespoons grated Parmesan cheese
½ teaspoon grated nutmeg
½ teaspoon dried thyme
Salt to taste (optional)
Freshly ground black pepper to taste

Serves 4 to 6

In a large skillet, sauté the zucchini, bell pepper, and onion in the olive oil and butter until the onion is translucent.

In a medium bowl, beat the eggs until frothy, then stir in the cheeses, nutmeg, thyme, salt, and black pepper. Pour the mixture evenly into the skillet and shake it into place.

When the bottom is formed and browned, put a large heatproof plate over the skillet, flip, then slide the frittata back into the skillet to cook the top. If you do not feel confident enough to do this, put the skillet under the broiler for 3 to 4 minutes (be sure the skillet has a flameproof handle).

BROCCOLI CHEESE FRITTATA

Frittata di Broccoli e Formaggio

½ head fresh broccoli, chopped (or 1 10-ounce package frozen
  chopped broccoli)
1 red bell pepper, cored, seeded, and diced
1 medium onion, thinly sliced
3 tablespoons olive oil
3 tablespoons unsalted butter
8 large eggs
1 cup shredded low-fat cheese
2 tablespoons grated Parmesan cheese
½ teaspoon grated nutmeg
½ teaspoon dried thyme
Salt to taste (optional)
Freshly ground black pepper to taste

Serves 4 to 6

In a large skillet, sauté the broccoli, bell pepper, and onion in the olive oil
and butter until the onion is translucent.

In a medium bowl, beat the eggs until frothy, then stir in the cheeses,
nutmeg, thyme, salt, and black pepper. Pour the mixture evenly into the
skillet and shake it into place.

When the bottom is formed and browned, put a large heatproof plate over
the skillet, flip, then slide the frittata back into the skillet to cook the top. If
you do not feel confident enough to do this, put the skillet under the broiler
for 3 to 4 minutes (be sure the skillet has a flameproof handle).

OVEN-BAKED POTATOES
Patate Arrosto

The bonus of putting a roast in the oven is the potatoes that cook alongside. I enjoy the crispness of the potatoes, the flavor of the olive oil, and the bits of onion.

As far as I'm concerned, the longer in the oven, the better. Since temperatures vary for different roasts, the potatoes can be added a little later.

4 to 6 potatoes, scrubbed but not peeled, thickly sliced
2 tablespoons olive oil
1 tablespoon unsalted butter, melted
1 medium onion, sliced
1 teaspoon ground rosemary
Freshly ground black pepper to taste
Salt to taste (optional)

Serves 4 to 6

Put all the ingredients in a large bowl and toss them. Place alongside a roast about 1½ hours before it is done. If cooking the potatoes alone, place them in a baking dish and roast at 400°F for 1 hour 15 minutes or longer, to desired tenderness (time can be shortened if potatoes are parboiled or slightly micro-waved).

POTATO CROQUETTES
Crocchette di Patate

The world loves potatoes fixed almost any way, whether plain, mashed, fried, boiled, or roasted. Here is a popular Italian recipe to add to your repertoire.

When Gran or Mom made these, they were eaten as fast as they were prepared, which meant that there were fewer for dinner!

2 pounds potatoes, unpeeled
2 large eggs or 4 large egg whites, beaten
2 ounces grated Parmesan cheese
2 tablespoons chopped fresh Italian parsley
Pinch nutmeg
½ teaspoon white pepper
Salt to taste (optional)
Chopped ham, salami, mozzarella cheese (optional)
1 cup bread crumbs
Olive oil for frying

Serves 4 to 6

In a stockpot, boil the potatoes until tender, peel if desired, and mash. Add the eggs, Parmesan cheese, parsley, nutmeg, pepper, salt, and optional ingredients as desired.

Mix together and form into sausage shapes (about 4 by 2 inches). Roll in the bread crumbs and refrigerate to firm up.

In a large skillet, fry the croquettes in olive oil until golden brown.

STUFFED TATERS
Patate Ripiene

8 baking potatoes, scrubbed
Olive oil
1 bunch scallions, sliced
1 tablespoon prepared horseradish
1 teaspoon dried oregano
1 teaspoon hot sauce
1 teaspoon Worcestershire sauce
⅛ teaspoon white pepper
2 cups shredded cheese

Serves 8

Preheat the oven to 425°F. Coat the potatoes with olive oil and bake for 1 hour 15 minutes. Cut in half lengthwise and scoop out two thirds of the flesh and place in a bowl. Put the shells under the broiler for 3 to 5 minutes.

Mix the scallions, horseradish, oregano, hot sauce, Worcestershire sauce, and pepper with half of the potato flesh. (The rest can be frozen for later use in soups, stews, croquettes.)

Stuff the shells and bake at 425°F for 15 to 20 minutes. After about 12 minutes, take the potatoes out and sprinkle with the cheese. Return to the oven for 5 minutes.

ROASTED POTATOES
Patate in Padella

Pan-roasted potatoes, even without roasted meat, were a perennial favorite in our family. Crusted with herbs and bathed in olive oil, they rival the best French fries for taste.

¼ cup olive oil
Juice of ½ lemon
2 teaspoons dried rosemary
Salt to taste (optional)
Freshly ground black pepper to taste
8 to 10 small red Bliss potatoes, quartered

Serves 4 to 6

Preheat the oven to 400°F. In a large bowl, mix the oil with the lemon juice, rosemary, salt, and pepper. Toss the potatoes in the mixture, place in a baking pan, and roast for 90 minutes. Turn the potatoes occasionally during the roasting time. (The potatoes can be partially cooked in the microwave to reduce the roasting time.)

PEPPERS AND POTATOES
Peroni e Patate

Italian frying peppers have a mild, sweet flavor that works beautifully with potatoes.

2 cloves garlic, chopped
1 medium onion, sliced
¼ cup olive oil
½ teaspoon dried thyme
1 teaspoon fennel seeds
Freshly ground black pepper to taste
Salt to taste (optional)
2 tablespoons tomato paste
½ cup water
1 pound long green frying peppers, seeded and cut into strips
6 unpeeled medium potatoes, halved and sliced

Serves 4 to 6

In a large skillet, sauté the garlic and onion in the olive oil until translucent. Add the thyme, fennel seeds, black pepper, and salt; mix the tomato paste with the water and stir in. Add the green peppers and potatoes, cover, and cook over low heat until the potatoes are tender, 15 to 20 minutes.

FLAVORED RICE
Risotto

*A*rborio, Italian short-grained rice, has a pronounced nutty flavor, and a porousness that readily absorbs the flavors of the ingredients it's cooked with.

1 thick slice prosciutto, chopped
1 tablespoon olive oil
3 cups chicken broth (recipe on page 15)
1 cup Italian short-grain rice
¼ teaspoon ground rosemary
Freshly ground black pepper to taste
Salt to taste (optional)
2 tablespoons unsalted butter
1 cup peas
2 tablespoons grated Romano cheese

Serves 4

In a large skillet, sauté the prosciutto in the olive oil for a few minutes, then add 2 cups of the broth and all of the rice. Add the rosemary, pepper, and salt and bring to a boil.

Add the remaining cup of broth and simmer, stirring, for approximately 20 minutes. When the rice is almost cooked, add the butter, peas, and cheese. Cook another few minutes until the peas are tender.

RICE AND PEAS
Risi e Bisi

My version of this traditional Venetian speciality is thicker than most and makes a terrific side dish.

1 small onion, diced
¼ cup (½ stick) unsalted butter
1 tablespoon chopped fresh Italian parsley
3 cups chicken broth (recipe on page 15)
1½ cups long-grain rice
1½ cups frozen peas
6 ounces Parmesan cheese, grated
Freshly ground black pepper to taste

Serves 6 to 8

In a large skillet, gently sauté the onion in the butter until soft. Add the parsley, broth, and rice. When the rice is almost cooked, add the peas and cook another 5 minutes. Add the grated Parmesan cheese and pepper and mix well.

CABBAGE WITH RICE

Cavolo con Riso

½ **cup raisins**
½ **cup cider vinegar**
1 head cabbage, shredded and cooked
2 cups cooked rice
½ **teaspoon turmeric**
2 tablespoons pine nuts
1 tablespoon brown sugar
Salt to taste (optional)
Freshly ground black pepper to taste

Serves 4 to 6

Preheat the oven to 350°F. In a small bowl, soak the raisins in the vinegar. Grease a baking dish and add half of the cabbage. When the raisins are plump, drain, reserving the vinegar.

In a medium bowl, mix the rice, turmeric, pine nuts, raisins, brown sugar, salt, and pepper together. Spread the mixture over the cabbage, then cover with the remaining cabbage; drizzle the top with the reserved vinegar. Bake, uncovered, for 35 to 45 minutes.

CHAPTER 6

❦

Fish
Pesce

Some of us remember those little fish that marked every Friday on the church calendar that hung on the inside of the pantry door. Yes, we had fish every Friday dinner and fish throughout Lent. But realize that we aren't just talking fish cakes with carrots and peas. We are talking anything but penance.

There was calamari, majestically sautéed and served atop a bed of linguine. Sole, smeared with pesto and baked to perfection. Leftover clam cakes that I would dip in a pool of mayonnaise as my late-night snack.

Crabs with pasta sauce were my brother's favorite. When he was seven or eight, he would meticulously pick all the meat out of the shells, then suck the shells of juice and try to wipe his hands on me.

Funny how the rest of the world has caught up with Mom's church calendar. Fish consumption is at an all-time high.

JOSIE'S FISH CAKES
Polpette di Pesce alla Giuseppina

I love the cracklin' taste of a good fish cake in which the fish is the main ingredient, and that's why I love Josie's recipe. The blend of flavors is just right, and they are fried in olive oil, which adds even more flavor.

2 pounds any white-fleshed fish, cooked and flaked
1 small onion, minced and cooked
2 cups mashed potatoes
4 large egg whites
1 tablespoon fresh lemon juice
3 tablespoons mayonnaise
2 tablespoons drained small capers
½ teaspoon dried thyme
½ teaspoon white pepper
½ cup bread crumbs
Olive oil for frying

Serves 4 to 6

Mix all the ingredients together except the bread crumbs and olive oil. Form into 8 large patties and dredge in the bread crumbs to coat.

In a large skillet, fry the fish cakes in olive oil, turning once, until golden. Drain on paper towels.

SCALLOPS HUNTER STYLE

Canestrelli alla Cacciatora

1 small onion, chopped
1 clove garlic, crushed
½ stalk celery, chopped
2 tablespoons olive oil
1 pound bay scallops or sea scallops, cut into quarters
6 ripe plum tomatoes, chopped
½ teaspoon dried sage
½ teaspoon dried rosemary
4 ounces *whole* button mushrooms
½ cup white wine
Freshly ground black pepper to taste
Salt to taste (optional)

Serves 4

In a medium skillet, sauté the onion, garlic, and celery in the olive oil until soft. Add the scallops and sauté lightly until opaque; *do not overcook*. Remove the scallops and keep warm.

Add the tomatoes, sage, rosemary, mushrooms, wine, pepper, and salt to the skillet. Boil over high heat for 4 to 7 minutes until reduced slightly.

Return the scallops to the skillet; remove from the heat to marry with the sauce. Serve immediately.

Genoese Fish Stew

Zuppa di Pesce Genovese

This stew is so easy and so elegant, particularly if you serve it in a beautiful tureen. The one I use belonged to my grandmother. Walnut oil gives the stew an unusual flavor.

2 to 2½ pounds assorted fish (cod fillets, sea bass, red snapper, monkfish)
2 cloves garlic
1 onion, chopped
½ cup walnut oil
2 anchovy fillets
2 tablespoons chopped fresh Italian parsley
8 ripe plum tomatoes, chopped
¾ cup dry white wine
1 bay leaf
Freshly ground black pepper to taste
Salt to taste (optional)
1 cup fish stock or water

Serves 4

Cut the fish into large bite-size pieces.

In a large skillet, sauté the garlic and onion in the walnut oil until soft. Add the anchovies, which should blend into the oil, then add the tomatoes, wine, bay leaf, pepper and salt. Cover and cook for 5 minutes.

Add the stock or water and the fish. Cook, covered, at a slow simmer for approximately 15 minutes, or until the fish is cooked. Sprinkle on parsley and serve with *Crostini* (see page 13).

SCALLOPS MARINARA

Canestrelli alla Marinara

One of my favorite ways to enjoy this dish is over a large plate of linguine.

1 small onion, chopped
1 clove garlic, crushed
2 tablespoons olive oil
1 pound bay scallops or sea scallops, cut into quarters
½ teaspoon dried sage
½ cup white wine
6 ripe plum tomatoes, chopped
1 teaspoon lemon juice
¼ teaspoon white pepper
1 tablespoon chopped fresh Italian parsley
Salt to taste (optional)

Serves 4

In a medium skillet, sauté the onion and garlic in the olive oil until soft. Add the scallops and sauté lightly until opaque; *do not overcook*. Remove the scallops and keep warm.

Add the sage, wine, tomatoes, lemon juice, pepper, parsley, and salt to the skillet. Boil over high heat for 3 to 5 minutes until reduced slightly.

Return the scallops to the skillet; remove from the heat to marry with the sauce. Serve immediately.

SHRIMP MARINARA

Gamberetti alla Marinara

Follow the recipe for Scallops Marinara (above), replacing the scallops with large shrimp, shelled and deveined.

BAKED STUFFED SHRIMP

Gamberi Ripiene al Forno

16 jumbo shrimp, shelled and deveined (keep tails intact)
3 tablespoons extra-virgin olive oil
¾ cup bread crumbs
1 clove garlic, minced
1 tablespoon chopped fresh Italian parsley
½ teaspoon ground oregano
½ teaspoon white pepper
Salt to taste (optional)
1 tablespoon fresh lemon juice
Lemon wedges

Serves 4

Preheat the oven to 450°F. Butterfly the shrimp and lay on a baking sheet. In a medium bowl, mix the oil, bread crumbs, garlic, parsley, oregano, pepper, salt, and lemon juice. Spoon onto the shrimp.

Bake for about 6 minutes, or until the shrimp are opaque. Then run under the broiler just until the topping is brown and crisp. Serve immediately with lemon wedges.

SCAMPI OR SHRIMP WITH GARLIC

Scampi o Gamberi all'Aglio

Scampi are a variety of crustacean from the Mediterranean. Although some restaurants in America list "Shrimp Scampi" on the menu, shrimp are most commonly used. This is the best classic recipe.

2 pounds scampi or large shrimp
2 tablespoons unsalted butter
2 tablespoons olive oil
1 bay leaf
2 to 3 garlic cloves, minced
½ teaspoon white pepper
½ tablespoon fresh lemon juice
Salt to taste (optional)
2 tablespoons chopped fresh Italian parsley

Serves 4 to 6 as a main dish or 6 to 8 as an appetizer

Remove the scampi meat from the shells or shell and devein the shrimp.

In a large skillet, heat the butter and olive oil with the bay leaf. Add the scampi or shrimp and lightly sauté for 2 to 3 minutes. Add the garlic, pepper, lemon juice, and salt, then remove the bay leaf and discard. Add the parsley and continue cooking for 3 minutes or longer, until the scampi are opaque.

Swordfish with Green Sauce

Pesce Spada in Salsa Verde

4 swordfish steaks
2 tablespoons olive oil
1 recipe Green Sauce (page 41)
1 lemon, sliced, for garnish

Serves 4

Preheat the oven to 375°F. Brush the fish with the olive oil and place in a baking dish. Bake for about 10 minutes, then brush green sauce onto each steak and continue to bake another 8 to 10 minutes, or until cooked through.

Garnish with lemon slices.

Sautéed Squid

Calamari in Padella

To many, squid is a rubbery mass that serves as a base for a deep-fried coating and a thick layer of cocktail sauce. But in this recipe, squid takes its rightful place as the centerpiece of an especially flavorful dish—and yes, it is perfect served over a steamy plate of pasta.

3 cloves garlic
3 tablespoons olive oil
1 tablespoon unsalted butter
1 pound cleaned squid, cut into bite-size pieces
½ cup dry white wine
3 tablespoons chopped fresh Italian parsley
½ teaspoon crushed red pepper flakes
Freshly ground black pepper to taste
Salt to taste (optional)

Serves 4 to 6

In a medium skillet, sauté the garlic in the oil and butter and discard when golden. Add the squid and sauté for 3 to 5 minutes. Remove the squid and add the wine, parsley, red pepper, black pepper, and salt to the skillet; reduce briskly. Pour the liquid over the squid and serve.

SQUID SALAD
Insalata di Calamari

3 cloves garlic, thinly sliced
2 stalks fennel or celery with leaves, thinly sliced
3 tablespoons olive oil
1 pound cleaned squid, cut into bite-size pieces
2 tablespoons fresh lemon juice
12 whole black olives, pitted
1 tablespoon drained small capers
½ teaspoon crushed red pepper flakes
1 teaspoon dried thyme
2 tablespoons chopped fresh Italian parsley
Freshly ground black pepper to taste
Salt to taste (optional)

Serves 4 to 6

Place a large mixing bowl in the refrigerator to chill.

In a large skillet, sauté the garlic and fennel (or celery) briefly in the oil; add the squid and stir. Cook for *only* 4 to 5 minutes; the squid will turn opaque. Remove from the heat; *do not overcook*.

Place the squid in the chilled bowl and mix in the lemon juice, olives, capers, red pepper flakes, thyme, parsley, black pepper, and salt. Toss and cover. Refrigerate for a few hours prior to serving.

THE DEVIL'S LOBSTER

Aragosta alla Fra Diavolo

1 small onion, minced
2 tablespoons olive oil
2 tablespoons unsalted butter
2 cups canned plum tomatoes, drained and chopped
½ cup bread crumbs
2 cloves garlic, minced
1 teaspoon dried oregano
½ teaspoon crushed red pepper flakes
2 tablespoons chopped fresh Italian parsley
½ cup dry white wine
¼ teaspoon white pepper
Salt to taste (optional)
4 1¼-pound lobsters, split and cleaned
1 lemon, cut into wedges

Serves 4

Preheat the oven to 350°F. In a medium skillet, sauté the onion in the olive oil and butter until soft. Add the tomatoes, bread crumbs, garlic, oregano, red pepper flakes, parsley, wine, pepper, and salt. Simmer for 6 to 8 minutes.

Cover each lobster (split side up) with the sauce, heaping it on if necessary. Place in a large baking dish and bake for 15 to 18 minutes. Serve one lobster per person. Serve with lemon wedges.

Cooking with Love, Italian Style

LOBSTER TAIL WITH VERMOUTH SAUCE

Coda di Aragosta in Salsa di Vino

The sweet lobster meat in the tails is nudged to perfection with this light vermouth sauce.

½ cup chopped scallions
2 tablespoons olive oil
2 tablespoons unsalted butter
2 tablespoons chopped fresh Italian parsley
1 teaspoon dried oregano
¼ teaspoon white pepper
1 tablespoon drained small capers
¼ cup white vermouth
4 lobster tails, split, with meat exposed

Serves 4

Preheat the oven to 350°F. In a small skillet, sauté the scallions in the olive oil and butter until soft. Add the parsley, oregano, pepper, capers, and white vermouth, stir, and simmer for 5 minutes. Spoon onto oven-ready lobster tails and bake for 12 to 15 minutes, or until cooked through.

Spoon on any remaining sauce and serve.

TUSCAN STUFFED FILLET OF SOLE

Filetti di Sogliola Ripieni alla Toscana

White beans and a touch of orange zest work beautifully with sole or any mild-flavored whitefish.

1 small onion, minced
2 tablespoons olive oil
1 tablespoon unsalted butter
½ cup bread crumbs
1 cup cooked and drained white beans
1 tablespoon grated orange zest
½ teaspoon ground rosemary
⅛ teaspoon grated nutmeg
½ cup dry white wine
1 large egg white, beaten
½ teaspoon white pepper
Salt to taste (optional)
8 medium sole fillets
1 pound fresh spinach, chopped and cooked (or 1 10-ounce package
   frozen chopped spinach, cooked)

Serves 4 to 6

Preheat the oven to 400°F. In a medium skillet, sauté the onion in the olive oil and butter until translucent. Remove from the heat and mix in the bread crumbs, beans, orange zest, rosemary, nutmeg, white wine, egg white, pepper, and salt. Mash the beans with a spoon as you mix.

Spread at least 1 tablespoon of this mixture on each fish fillet and roll from end to end. Place in an oiled baking dish, cover with foil, and bake for about 10 minutes. Remove the foil and bake an additional 4 to 6 minutes, or until cooked.

When ready to serve, make a bed of cooked spinach on each dinner plate. Place a stuffed fillet in the center and serve.

FILLET OF SOLE GENOA STYLE

Sogliola alla Genovese

Once again, an example of how in Italian cooking less is more. The seasoning enhances the flavor of the fish, for a dish that is ready in minutes.

1 tablespoon Pesto (recipe on page 57)
1 tablespoon olive oil
4 large sole fillets
Lemon slices, for garnish

Serves 4

Preheat the oven to 375°F. In a cup, mix the pesto and olive oil. Place the fish in a greased baking dish and brush the mixture on each fillet. Bake for 18 to 20 minutes, or until the fish is flaky. Garnish with lemon slices.

FISH STEW

Cioppino

This is a big, hearty fisherman's stew. Serve with plenty of Italian bread to "drink" and taste every drop!

2 pounds assorted fish (sea bass, monkfish, etc.)
12 ounces shrimp
12 hard-shell clams
12 mussels
3 crabs or 2 small lobsters
3 cloves garlic
2 onions, chopped
1 carrot, chopped
3 tablespoons olive oil
4 ounces mushrooms, sliced
3 cups fish stock or water
1 28 to 32-ounce can Italian plum tomatoes with their juice, crushed
1 cup dry white wine
Juice of ½ lemon
1 anchovy fillet, chopped
½ teaspoon dried basil
¼ teaspoon dried oregano
¼ teaspoon crushed red pepper flakes
Freshly ground black pepper to taste
Salt to taste (optional)
1 tablespoon pesto (optional)
2 tablespoons chopped fresh Italian parsley

Serves 6

Wash all of the fish, shell and devein the shrimp, and scrub the clams, mussels, and crabs.

In a large stockpot, sauté the garlic, onions, and carrot in the olive oil until the onions are soft. Discard the garlic. Add the mushrooms and the stock or water, bring to a boil, then lower the heat to a simmer.

Remove 1 cup of the liquid and pour it into another stockpot. Add the scrubbed clams, mussels, and crabs (or lobsters) to this pot. Cook over medium-high heat for 5 to 10 minutes, until the clams and mussels open.

Meanwhile, to the original pot, add the tomatoes and their juice, the wine, lemon juice, anchovy, basil, oregano, red pepper flakes, black pepper, and salt. Cover and simmer about 20 minutes. This is the perfect time to add a tablespoon of pesto (see page 57).

Remove the shellfish from the second stockpot and strain their juices through a cheesecloth. Discard any mussels and clams that do not open. Crack open the crabs or lobsters and pick out the meat. Add the strained juice and the uncooked fish to the main pot and cook, covered, for 20 minutes. Add the clams, mussels, crab or lobster meat, and mushrooms and cook 8 minutes longer, uncovered.

Transfer all the fish to a serving platter. Raise the heat, mix in the parsley, and reduce the sauce by approximately half its volume. Return the seafood to the pot and heat through.

MONKFISH

This fish, often referred to as "poor man's lobster," is also called angelfish, goosefish, and a variety of other names. Its firm white flesh has a sweet taste, which is enhanced here with lemon juice and onion.

1 large red onion, thinly sliced
2 tablespoons unsalted butter
2 tablespoons olive oil
Juice of ½ lemon
1 tablespoon white vinegar
½ teaspoon white pepper
½ teaspoon dried oregano
Salt to taste (optional)
4 monkfish fillets

Serves 4

(continued)

In a medium skillet, sauté the onion in the butter and olive oil until translucent. Add the lemon juice, vinegar, pepper, oregano, and salt to the skillet. Add the fish, cover, and cook for 5 minutes on each side, or until the fish is opaque.

BAKED BASS
Branzino al Forno

This is a simple, yet elegant enough dish for a party.

1 clove garlic, minced
6 ripe plum tomatoes, chopped
1 tablespoon unsalted butter
2 tablespoons olive oil
1 tablespoon fresh lemon juice
12 black olives, sliced
Freshly ground black pepper to taste
Salt to taste (optional)
4 bass fillets
6 tablespoons bread crumbs
Parsley sprigs, for garnish

Serves 4

Preheat the oven to 375°F. In a small skillet, briefly sauté the garlic and tomatoes in the butter and 1 tablespoon of the olive oil. Remove from the heat and add the lemon juice, olives, pepper, and salt.

Grease a baking dish that is large enough to hold the fish, and place the fillets in it, skin side up. Mix the bread crumbs with the remaining tablespoon of olive oil and spread on the fillets. Spoon on the tomato and olive mixture.

Bake for 25 to 30 minutes or until cooked. Garnish with parsley.

BAKED CLAMS
Vongole Gratinate

Be forewarned! Once you've made these baked clams with love and care in your own kitchen, you'll never settle for the restaurant version again.

36 hard-shell clams
2 cloves garlic, crushed
1 small onion, minced
2 tablespoons olive oil or more if needed
¾ cup bread crumbs
2 tablespoons chopped fresh Italian parsley
6 tablespoons grated Parmesan cheese
Juice of ½ lemon
½ teaspoon dried oregano
Freshly ground black pepper to taste
Salt to taste (optional)
2 lemons, cut into wedges

Serves 6

Preheat the oven to 425°F. Wash and scrub the clams. Place in a large covered saucepan with 2 tablespoons of water and steam until they open. Discard any that remain closed. Strain and reserve the pan liquid and remove the clams. Break off and discard one half shell from each clam. In the clam you will see a small greenish-brown sac, which should be cut out and discarded. Rinse the meat. Place the clams in their half shells on a baking sheet.

In a small skillet, sauté the garlic and onion in the olive oil, discarding the garlic when it becomes golden. Add the bread crumbs, reserved clam liquid, parsley, Parmesan cheese, lemon juice, oregano, pepper, and salt to the skillet. Add more oil if the mixture is very dry.

Top each clam with a mound of the mixture and bake for approximately 10 minutes, until lightly browned on top. *Do not overcook.* Serve with lemon wedges.

CLAM CAKES
Torta di Vongole

Make these ahead and reheat for a great first course or party hors d'oeuvres.

1½ cups all-purpose flour
3½ teaspoons baking powder
2 cups chopped clams
1 egg, beaten
1 teaspoon ground ginger
½ teaspoon grated nutmeg
½ teaspoon cayenne pepper
½ teaspoon dried oregano
1 tablespoon chopped fresh Italian parsley
¼ teaspoon white pepper
Salt to taste (optional)
1 tablespoon fresh lemon juice
1 cup clam juice
Vegetable oil for frying
Marinara sauce (recipe on page 67) or tartar sauce

Yields 3 to 4 dozen pieces, depending on size

In a large bowl, sift together the flour and baking powder, then mix in the clams. Add the egg, ginger, nutmeg, cayenne, oregano, parsley, pepper, salt, lemon juice, and clam juice and mix well.

In a deep fryer heat the oil to 375°F. Using 2 teaspoons, plunge one into the batter and use the other to push the batter into the hot oil. The clam cakes will puff up. Fry until the clam cakes turn golden, approximately 2 minutes, then turn over. Cook 1½ to 2 minutes more.

Transfer the clam cakes to paper towels to absorb the excess oil. Serve hot. Serve the simmering marinara sauce or tartar sauce over the clam cakes.

These clams cakes can be refrigerated for later use. To reheat, place them in a 350°F oven for 15 to 20 minutes or in an average microwave for 2½ to 3 minutes.

FISH WITH WHITE WINE

Pesce al Vino Bianco

1 bunch scallions, chopped
12 green olives, sliced
1 tablespoon unsalted butter
1 cup dry white wine
1 tablespoon drained small capers
Juice of ½ lemon
¼ teaspoon white pepper
2 tablespoons chopped fresh Italian parsley
4 fillets of your favorite fish
1 lemon, sliced, for garnish

Serves 4

In a large skillet, sauté the scallions and olives in the butter until soft. Add the wine, capers, lemon juice, pepper, and parsley; bring to a boil, then lower the heat to a simmer.

Immediately add the fish and cook for 5 to 8 minutes, when it should appear flaky. Remove the fish to a warm serving platter.

Reduce the sauce to about half, and pour over the fish. Garnish with lemon slices and serve.

CRABS WITH PASTA

Pasta al Granchio

When I was a little guy shopping with Mom at the local fishmonger, it was quite traumatic seeing live blue crabs go into the bag. How was I going to carry them? What if they got loose and turned the street into a horror movie? Would I later open the refrigerator door and have one leap out at me?

Needless to say, everyone was safe, and thanks to Mom's culinary talents, those crawlers were turned into a delectable treat that she used in a pasta sauce. We always searched out every bit of juice and meat in the shell.

Today you can buy shelled crabmeat, which is an acceptable substitute in this recipe. But if you can find whole live crabs, you're really in for a treat.

8 to 12 large hard-shell crabs, preferably blue claws
1 recipe for pasta (preferably linguine) with marinara sauce (page 67)

Serves 4 to 6

Using tongs, plunge the live crabs into a stockpot of boiling water. When they no longer thrash around, remove them and rinse them under running water, scrubbing the shells and removing any sand or grit.

After you've sautéed the onions and garlic for your marinara sauce, add the crabs to the recipe and finish making the sauce.

It is helpful, during the last 10 minutes of cooking time, to remove the crabs and break away or pull off the top shells. Discard the spongy, feather-looking material, including the yellowish stomach and digestive system. Return the crabs to the sauce and continue cooking. Suggested serving is two crabs each, on a bed of linguine.

BAKED CRAB LEGS
Gambe di Granchio al Forno

½ onion, minced
1 tablespoon unsalted butter
1 tablespoon olive oil
½ cup bread crumbs
Juice of ½ lemon
Freshly ground black pepper to taste
4 to 6 king crab legs
1 recipe Sautéed Spinach (page 88)

Serves 4 to 6

Preheat the oven to 425°F. In a small skillet, sauté the onion in the butter and olive oil until translucent. Add the bread crumbs, lemon juice, and pepper and mix thoroughly.

Crab meat should be exposed; crack the shells if necessary.

Place the crab legs in a baking dish and cover with the bread crumb mixture. Bake for 16 to 18 minutes or until browned.

Serve the crab legs on a bed of the hot spinach.

MUSSELS

Cozze

*M*y mother taught me that nature keeps the lids on these nutritious creatures to lock their goodness in. When you buy them, they should be alive and their shells tightly closed. After cooking, any mussels whose shells do not open when cooling should be discarded. The following recipe has touches of herbs that help the rich, earthy mussel flavor burst through. Serve with Italian bread or Crostini *(page 13)* to soak up all the delicious juice.

4 dozen mussels
½ cup fish stock or water
1 cup dry white wine
1 tablespoon fresh lemon juice
1 clove garlic crushed
¼ cup olive oil
1½ cups canned plum tomatoes with their juice, chopped
½ teaspoon dried thyme
¼ teaspoon dried basil
¼ teaspoon crushed red pepper flakes
Freshly ground black pepper to taste
Salt to taste (optional)
2 tablespoons chopped fresh Italian parsley

Serves 6 as an appetizer or 4 as a main course

Scrub and wash the mussels well. Put the stock, wine, and lemon juice in a stockpot and bring to a boil. Add the mussels, cover, and simmer for about 5 minutes, until they open. Remove the mussels, strain the liquid through cheesecloth, and throw out any mussels whose shells remain tightly closed.

In a large skillet, sauté the garlic in the olive oil. When the garlic is golden, add the tomatoes, thyme, basil, red pepper, black pepper, and salt and simmer for about 6 minutes. Add the strained liquid and cook another 4 minutes.

Add the mussels to the skillet and cook another 2 minutes, or until they are heated through. Add the parsley and serve.

BROILED TUNA WITH OLIVE DRESSING

Tonno ai ferri in Salsa di Olive

This topping has a spicy kick that still allows the taste of the fresh tuna to come through.

4 tuna steaks
3 tablespoons olive oil
12 black olives, pitted
2 tablespoons lemon juice
½ teaspoon fennel seeds
1 clove garlic
1 teaspoon dried rosemary
1 tablespoon chopped fresh Italian parsley
¼ teaspoon red pepper flakes
Freshly ground black pepper to taste
Salt to taste (optional)

Serves 4

Preheat the broiler. Brush the tuna with 1 tablespoon of the olive oil and broil for about 5 minutes on each side, or until the fish is opaque and flaky.

Meanwhile, put the remaining ingredients into a mini food processor or blender, add more oil if needed, and purée. Brush the dressing on the fish during the last few minutes of cooking time. Serve immediately.

CHAPTER 7

❧

Meat
Carne

*A*t the Italian table, meat is most often consumed in small quantities. Rather than being the centerpiece, it is part of the total presentation. That's one of the many reasons Italian cooking fits in so well with today's dietary guidelines.

Even when I fix guests my favorite beef wrapped with basil on special occasions, the serving portions are always small. And when I serve Aunt Ida's meatballs with capers, two or three are enough for an average serving. Often a taste is all that is needed to satisfy. And there is the additional benefit that expensive cuts like the filet mignon used in my beef with basil become affordable even on the strictest of budgets.

Italians love their veal dishes but I recommend that you not buy veal unless it is good quality. You can use chicken or turkey cutlets for recipes like my veal piccata. Of course, there is no replacing a veal shank full of marrow for osso buco. But that's a rare treat!

OVEN BEEF STEW

Garafolato

2 pounds beef stew meat, cut into 1-inch cubes
1 tablespoon olive oil
Salt to taste (optional)
Freshly ground black pepper to taste
1 clove garlic, minced
5 small onions (2 finely chopped, 2 sliced, 1 whole)
¾ teaspoon dried thyme
1 bay leaf
⅔ cup chopped fresh Italian parsley
3 cups beef stock
4 whole cloves
6 carrots, cut into 2-inch pieces
4 medium potatoes, unpeeled and cut into 2-inch pieces
About 1 pound rutabaga or turnips, peeled and cut into 2-inch pieces
  (2 cups)
½ pound fresh mushrooms, cut in half
2 tablespoons all-purpose flour
¼ cup cold water

Serves 4 to 6

Preheat the oven to 500°F. Place the beef cubes and oil in a Dutch oven or heavy flameproof casserole. Sprinkle with salt and pepper; add the garlic and chopped onions and mix. Brown the meat, uncovered, in the oven for 20 minutes.

Add the thyme, bay leaf, half of the parsley, and the beef stock; lower the oven temperature to 350°F, cover, and cook for 40 minutes.

Stick the cloves into the whole onion and add it and the sliced onions to the stew, along with the carrots, potatoes, and rutabaga. Cook, covered, for another 45 minutes. Add the mushrooms and cook 10 minutes longer.

Remove the stew from the oven. Mix the flour with the cold water, and stir into the stew. Simmer 5 to 8 minutes on top of the stove, until the gravy thickens slightly. Sprinkle with the remaining parsley before serving. Freeze half of the stew for another evening.

BEEF WRAPPED WITH BASIL

Manzo al Basilico

I often serve this recipe for extra-special occasions, like a New Year's Day dinner. My dinner guests seem to love this tenderest prime cut of meat infused with the tastes of basil and garlic. With it, I serve a sparking white Italian wine, even though red is more traditional with beef.

1 10-pound whole filet mignon, trimmed of all visible fat
1 recipe Pesto (page 57)
2 bunches fresh basil
Freshly ground black pepper to taste

Serves 12 to 14

Preheat the oven to 425°F. Tear off a large piece of aluminum foil or paper.

Place the meat in the center of the foil and smear pesto all over it. Press on the basil leaves, sprinkle with pepper, and wrap securely.

Place on a baking sheet and roast for 18 minutes for medium-rare.

Lower the oven temperature to 350°F and roast for approximately 75 to 90 minutes more, or until the meat thermometer reaches 130° for rare.

Remove the wrapping and pour the juices into a bowl. Defat the juices and serve along with the meat.

STUFFED BEEF
Braciole Ripiene

Braciole *is great on its own, but it is also a traditional ingredient in a slow-cooking tomato meat sauce (see page 68).*

3 tablespoons olive oil
1 small onion, minced
2 cloves garlic, minced
2 tablespoons grated Romano cheese
2 tablespoons chopped fresh Italian parsley
¼ cup white raisins, plumped in wine
¼ cup pine nuts
Freshly ground black pepper to taste
Salt to taste (optional)
1½ to 2 pounds beef top round steak, about ¼ inch thick, pounded
   thin
3 cups marinara sauce (recipe on page 67)

Serves 4 to 6

In a medium bowl, mix 2 tablespoons of the olive oil with the rest of the ingredients except the beef and tomato sauce.

Spread this filling over the steak. Roll up, jelly roll fashion, then tie securely with string. Can be cut into smaller pieces for easier handling.

Heat the remaining tablespoon of olive oil in a skillet and brown the *braciole*. Drain off any remaining oil and add the sauce. Simmer, covered, for 1½ to 2 hours, or until the meat is very tender. Remove the string before serving.

BEEF STEW ROMAN STYLE

Stufato alla Romana

1 slice prosciutto, about ⅛ inch thick, chopped
1 small onion, minced
2 stalks celery, chopped
1 tablespoon olive oil
2 pounds beef stew meat, cut into 1-inch cubes
¾ cup dry red wine
2 tablespoons tomato paste
2 cups beef stock
¼ teaspoon dried marjoram
1 clove garlic, minced
1 teaspoon lemon juice
Freshly ground black pepper to taste
Salt to taste (optional)

Serves 4 to 6

In a large skillet, sauté the prosciutto, onion, and celery in the olive oil. When
the onion is translucent, add the meat and brown quickly. Add the wine and
deglaze the skillet. (Deglazing loosens the pan drippings when you use wine
or stock; heat and scrape with a wooden spoon.) When the liquid has reduced,
mix the tomato paste with the beef stock and add to the skillet. Then add the
marjoram, garlic, lemon juice, pepper, and salt. Cover and simmer for 2 to
2½ hours, or until the meat is tender.

POT ROAST ROMAN STYLE

Stracotto alla Romana

This dish takes a little time, so you might want to start it on Sunday night for Monday night dinner. Even lesser cuts of meat are tender and flavorful when cooked "Roman style."

1 3 to 3½-pound pot roast (rump or eye of round)
3 tablespoons olive oil
2 white onions, chopped
4 cloves garlic, crushed
2 stalks celery, chopped
2 carrots, chopped
8 plum tomatoes, chopped
¼ teaspoon Worcestershire sauce
¾ cup dry red wine
1 cup beef stock
⅛ teaspoon sugar
Freshly ground black pepper to taste
Salt to taste (optional)

Serves 6

Brush the meat with 1 tablespoon of the olive oil, place the meat in a large skillet or Dutch oven, and brown on all sides over high heat. Remove the meat.

Reduce the heat and sauté the onions, garlic, celery, and carrots in the remaining 2 tablespoons of olive oil until soft. Add the rest of the ingredients, replace the meat, cover, and simmer for 2½ to 3 hours, or until the meat is very tender. During cooking, turn the meat several times and baste.

Remove the meat and defat the pan juices. Purée the vegetables in the juices and serve as a sauce with the sliced meat.

MOM'S BEEF AND PEPPERS

Manzo ai Peperoni della Mamma

On some Saturday afternoons Mom would make this extraordinary dish. My brother Andrew and I loved the flavors of the beef blended with the Italian frying peppers, both fried in olive oil. To us the steak could have been filet mignon. And those glistening pieces of orange and green peppers look great spilling out from between slices of freshly baked bread. I know it was fresh because while Mom was cooking the filling, Andrew and I had the job of fetching the bread hot from the bakery a few blocks away.

2 cloves garlic
¼ cup olive oil
1 large onion, thinly sliced
8 Italian frying peppers, cut into strips
1½ pounds lean chuck steak or sirloin, thinly sliced
¼ teaspoon dried oregano
⅛ teaspoon celery salt
⅛ teaspoon crushed red pepper flakes
Freshly ground black pepper to taste
Salt to taste (optional)
½ teaspoon fresh lemon juice
¼ teaspoon Worcestershire sauce

Serves 4 to 6

In a large skillet, sauté the garlic in the olive oil and discard when golden. Add the onion and peppers to the skillet and sauté until soft. Then add the beef (it may be browned separately, then added when cooked to eliminate excess fat). Add the oregano, celery salt, red pepper flakes, black pepper, salt, lemon juice, and Worcestershire sauce. Cover and cook over low heat until heated through (about 5 to 10 minutes).

Veal Marengo

Vitello Marengo

Here's another veal dish with a "second time around" bonus. Plan it as a party buffet dish that can be made ahead. It seems to get better with a little time. Don't we all!

4½ pounds stewing veal, cut into 1-inch cubes
½ cup all-purpose flour
2 cloves garlic, crushed
2 large onions, sliced
½ cup olive oil
2 cups dry white wine
1 35-ounce can Italian plum tomatoes, chopped, with their juice
2 green bell peppers, chopped
¾ teaspoon dried thyme
¾ teaspoon dried tarragon
1 bay leaf
Freshly ground black pepper to taste
Salt to taste (optional)
12 ounces mushrooms, sliced
1 tablespoon brown sugar
½ cup water (if needed)
½ cup chopped fresh Italian parsley

Serves 10 to 12

Preheat the oven to 350°F. Coat the veal with the flour. In a large skillet, sauté the garlic and onions in a little of the oil until soft. Add 3 to 4 more tablespoons of oil to the skillet and brown the veal. You will need to cook the veal in several batches; use more oil if needed.

When the veal pieces are browned, remove them to a large casserole, deglaze the pan with the wine, and add to the casserole.

Add the tomatoes and bell peppers to the casserole with the tomato juice. Add the thyme, tarragon, bay leaf, pepper, and salt. Cover and bake for 1 hour. Lower the oven temperature to 325°F and cook an additional 30 minutes. Stir.

Add the mushrooms to the casserole, stir in the brown sugar, and add the water, if needed, for juiciness. Continue baking for approximately 30 minutes longer. Remove the bay leaf.

Sprinkle with the parsley. Serve over rice or noodles.

VEAL WITH PROSCIUTTO

Saltimbocca alla Romana

This famous Roman dish literally means "jump in the mouth." In ancient times it was served as a quick bite; hence, the name.

8 veal cutlets, pounded thin
2 tablespoons olive oil
2 tablespoons unsalted butter
⅛ teaspoon ground sage
Freshly ground black pepper to taste
Salt to taste (optional)
8 thin slices prosciutto
1 lemon, thinly sliced, for garnish

Serves 4

Preheat the broiler. In a large skillet, sauté the veal lightly in the oil and butter. Place on a baking sheet and dust with the sage, pepper, and salt.

Top each slice of veal with a slice of prosciutto. Place under the broiler, farthest from direct heat, until the prosciutto is limp. Garnish with lemon slices and serve.

VEAL PICCATA

Piccata di Vitello

Although traditionally made with veal, this recipe works just as well with chicken or turkey cutlets pounded thin. This dish is especially popular with an increasing number of my friends who want a dinner that is not too filling or overbearing.

1½ pounds veal cutlets, pounded thin
¼ cup all-purpose flour
2 tablespoons olive oil
¼ cup unsalted butter or margarine
¾ cup dry white wine
½ cup fresh lemon juice (about 3 lemons)
1 teaspoon grated lemon zest
⅛ teaspoon dried sage
½ teaspoon white pepper
Salt to taste (optional)
1 tablespoon drained small capers (optional)
1 lemon, thinly sliced, for garnish
2 tablespoons chopped fresh Italian parsley, for garnish

Serves 4 to 6

Dust the veal cutlets lightly with flour. Heat the oil and butter in a large skillet, sauté the veal lightly, and remove to a heated platter.

Add the wine to the skillet and stir over medium to high heat. Add the lemon juice, lemon zest, sage, pepper, salt, and capers.

Continue stirring until the sauce is reduced. The lemon flavor should be the most pronounced; if it is not, add more juice.

Turn off the heat and return the veal to the skillet long enough to bathe in the lemon sauce.

Garnish the platter or individual plates with lemon slices and sprinkle parsley over all.

VEAL STEW

Spezzatino di Vitello

The great thing about making a big pot of stew is that you have another meal for another day. This recipe freezes well, and some people say it tastes even better the second time around.

2 cloves garlic, whole
½ cup olive oil
½ cup all-purpose flour
4 pounds stewing veal, cut into 1-inch pieces
1 onion, chopped
1 cup dry white wine
1 28-ounce can peeled tomatoes, chopped, with their juice
2 cups chicken broth (recipe on page 15)
¾ teaspoon dried thyme
2 bay leaves
Freshly ground black pepper to taste
Salt to taste (optional)
2 tablespoons chopped fresh Italian parsley, for garnish

Serves 8 to 10

In a large skillet, sauté the garlic in the olive oil until golden, then discard.

Generously flour the veal, add to the skillet with the onion, and quickly brown. Drain off any remaining oil and deglaze the skillet with the wine. (Deglazing loosens the pan drippings when you use wine or stock; heat and scrape with a wooden spoon.)

Add the tomatoes, broth, thyme, bay leaves, pepper, and salt to the veal. Simmer, covered, for 1 hour, stirring occasionally. Uncover and continue to simmer for an additional 50 minutes to 1 hour.

Discard the bay leaves before serving and sprinkle with chopped parsley.

VEAL SHANKS WITH RICE

Ossobuco

If I had to choose a dream meal, it probably would be veal falling off the bone, possibly served on a bed of risotto. And there's the bonus of the marrow that's in the veal shin bone, which you dig out with tiny forks and spread on bread. What a feast!

6 large veal shanks, 3 inches thick by 4–4½ inches wide (if small, allow
  2 per person)
½ cup all-purpose flour
2 tablespoons unsalted butter
2 tablespoons olive oil
1 cup dry white wine
2 cups beef stock
2 cups canned Italian plum tomatoes, drained and slightly crushed
⅛ teaspoon dried sage
Freshly ground black pepper to taste
Salt to taste (optional)
1 tablespoon grated lemon zest
3 cups cooked rice
Italian parsley sprigs, for garnish

Serves 6

Roll the veal shanks in the flour. Melt the butter with the oil in a skillet large enough to hold all the shanks in one layer. Add the shanks and brown them on all sides over medium-high heat.

    Lower the heat and pour in ¼ cup of the wine and ¼ cup of the stock. Cover and cook at a slow simmer for 40 minutes.

    Remove the shanks and defat the pan juices. Add the tomatoes to the juices in the skillet with the remainder of the stock and the sage, pepper, and salt. Combine.

    Return the shanks to the skillet and pour in the remainder of the wine. Cover and continue to cook for 1¾ to 2 hours, making sure that the contents do not boil but simmer very slowly. The meat should be very tender, so use tongs to remove the shanks to a warm platter when done.

Sprinkle a little of the lemon zest on each shank. Turn up the heat, add the chopped parsley, and reduce the sauce by half of its volume. Place each shank on an individual serving plate and encircle it with rice. Spoon on the sauce, criss-crossing over the meat. Garnish with parsley sprigs and serve.

ROAST VEAL WITH CAPER SAUCE

Vitello Arrosto in Salsa di Capperi

¼ teaspoon ground dried rosemary
1 tablespoon olive oil
1 3 to 3½-pound veal roast

CAPER SAUCE
1½ tablespoons unsalted butter or margarine
1½ tablespoons all-purpose flour
1 cup 1% low-fat milk
4 teaspoons finely chopped capers
Dash of bitters
½ cup fresh lemon juice
1 cup chicken broth (recipe on page 15)
1 teaspoon Dijon mustard
¼ teaspoon dried ground rosemary
¼ teaspoon white pepper
2 tablespoons chopped fresh Italian parsley

Serves 6 to 8

Preheat the oven to 400°F. Mix the rosemary and 1 tablespoon of the olive oil and liberally brush on the veal.

Place the veal on a roasting pan and roast for 40 minutes. Lower the oven temperature to 350°F and continue to roast until the internal temperature of the meat is approximately 160°F.

Meanwhile, in a small saucepan, make the caper sauce: Melt the butter, add the flour, and cook until golden, constantly stirring. Slowly blend in the milk, then add the capers, bitters, lemon juice, broth, mustard, rosemary, and pepper. When well blended, add the parsley.

Slice the meat and serve the caper sauce on the side.

CHEESE-STUFFED VEAL CHOPS

Cotolette alla Valdostana

Use only the best-quality ingredients for a symphony of flavors—a real masterpiece.

4 large veal chops
8 slices fontina cheese
1 cup bread crumbs
¼ teaspoon ground sage
¼ teaspoon grated nutmeg
2 tablespoons grated Romano cheese
1 tablespoon chopped fresh Italian parsley
Freshly ground black pepper to taste
Salt to taste (optional)
½ cup flour
2 large egg whites, beaten
2 tablespoons unsalted butter
3 tablespoons olive oil, or more as needed

Serves 4

Slice the chops in half horizontally up to the bone. Then layer 2 cheese slices inside each chop, keeping about ½ inch from the edges. Pound the chops slightly, using harder blows around the edges to help "seal."

In a shallow bowl, mix the bread crumbs with the sage, nutmeg, Romano cheese, parsley, pepper, and salt. Place the flour on a plate. Press the chops into the flour, then dip into the egg whites. Dredge in the bread crumb mixture to coat.

In a large skillet, gently sauté the chops in the butter and olive oil until golden tan, 5 to 8 minutes each side, depending on the thickness. Serve.

STUFFED BREAST OF VEAL

Panzetta

When I was growing up, I would eat only the end cut of panzetta. *Nowadays, it seems that the whole veal breast is much meatier and leaner. The stuffing and accompanying vegetables make this a satisfying dish for an early Sunday supper.*

1 pound sausage meat
1 small onion, chopped
2 tablespoons olive oil
1 cup bread crumbs
¼ cup grated Parmesan cheese
½ teaspoon dried ground rosemary
2 large egg whites, slightly beaten
½ cup dry white wine
1 tablespoon chopped fresh Italian parsley
Freshly ground black pepper to taste
Salt to taste (optional)
1 3 to 4-pound breast of veal, with pocket for stuffing

Serves 4 to 6

Preheat the oven to 350°F. In a large skillet, briskly sauté the sausage meat until just browned and remove to a bowl. Discard any drippings from the skillet.

In the same skillet, sauté the onion in the olive oil until translucent, then add to the bowl along with the bread crumbs, cheese, rosemary, egg whites, wine, parsley, pepper, and salt. Mix together.

Stuff the mixture into the veal breast and truss (tie with kitchen twine). Wrap the remaining stuffing in a foil packet and bake along with veal.

Roast for 2½ hours. Slice and serve.

ROSA'S VEAL ROLLS

Spiedini

The problem with making these veal rolls is that they seem to disappear as you fry them. So, keep the kitchen off limits while you're cooking!

1 tablespoon unsalted butter
3 tablespoons olive oil
3 tablespoons bread crumbs
2 tablespoons grated Parmesan cheese
¼ teaspoon dried sage
1 tablespoon chopped fresh Italian parsley
Freshly ground black pepper to taste
Salt to taste (optional)
1 pound veal cutlets, pounded thin and cut into 3-inch-square pieces
Several bay leaves
1 onion, quartered and layers separated

Serves 4 to 6

In a small bowl, mix the butter, 1 tablespoon of the olive oil, the bread crumbs, cheese, sage, parsley, pepper, and salt.

Spread the mixture over the veal pieces, then roll them up, jelly roll fashion. Place on a skewer, followed by a bay leaf and a piece of onion. Put 4 veal rolls on each skewer, alternating with bay leaves and onion.

In a large skillet, briefly sauté the completed skewers in the remaining olive oil on both sides until golden. Drain and serve.

Oven Method: Roast at 375°F for 12 to 15 minutes, then place under the broiler for a minute or two.

Veal Pizzaiola
Vitello alla Pizzaiola

This traditional Italian veal recipe can also be made with chicken or turkey cutlets.

1½ pounds veal cutlets, pounded thin
¼ cup olive oil
¼ cup (½ stick) unsalted butter
1 small onion, chopped
½ pound mushrooms, sliced
½ cup dry white wine
1½ cups marinara sauce (recipe on page 67)
¼ teaspoon dried oregano
Freshly ground black pepper to taste
Salt to taste (optional)
1 tablespoon chopped fresh Italian parsley

Serves 4 to 6

In a large skillet, sauté the veal in the oil and butter for approximately 3 minutes on each side. Remove when cooked to a heated platter. In the same skillet, sauté the onion and mushrooms. When the onion is translucent, add the wine, marinara sauce, oregano, pepper, and salt.

Simmer for 4 to 5 minutes, then pour over the veal. Sprinkle with parsley and serve.

VEAL MILANESE

Vitello alla Milanese

¼ teaspoon dried sage
Freshly ground black pepper to taste
Salt to taste (optional)
1 cup bread crumbs
1½ pounds veal cutlets, pounded thin
2 large eggs, beaten
¼ cup olive oil
¼ cup (½ stick) unsalted butter
1 lemon, cut into wedges, for garnish
Parsley sprigs, for garnish

Serves 4 to 6

Mix the sage, pepper, salt, and bread crumbs together in a shallow dish. Dip the veal into the egg, then dredge in the bread crumb mixture (making sure the meat is evenly coated).

In a large skillet, sauté the veal in the olive oil and butter on both sides until golden. Garnish with lemon wedges and parsley sprigs.

PORK CHOPS WITH FENNEL

Cotolette di Maiale al Finocchio

The fennel seeds in this recipe add a wonderful flavor and aroma.

4 large, thick, lean pork chops or 8 boneless pork cutlets
¼ cup all-purpose flour
1 tablespoon unsalted butter
2 tablespoons olive oil
¾ cup red wine
1 tablespoon tomato paste
⅛ teaspoon sugar
1 clove garlic, minced
¾ teaspoon fennel seeds
Juice of ½ lemon
Freshly ground black pepper to taste
Salt to taste (optional)
2 tablespoons chopped celery leaves

Serves 4

Dust the pork chops in the flour.

Heat the butter and oil in a large skillet and sauté the chops on both sides until thoroughly cooked. Remove them to a warm platter. If necessary, defat remaining juices in the skillet, then add the wine and deglaze. Stir in the tomato paste and sugar.

Add the garlic, fennel seeds, lemon juice, pepper, and salt. Reduce the sauce slightly over high heat, stirring constantly. Remove from the heat and return the pork to the skillet to bathe in the sauce. Sprinkle on chopped celery leaves and serve.

Baked Pork Chops and Sauerkraut

Cotolette di Maiale ai Cravti

My mother made this dish at least once a month when I was growing up. I've never been certain if this was an Italian family dish or a recipe borrowed from a German neighbor.

2 pounds loin pork chops
½ cup finely chopped tart apple
2 tablespoons unsalted butter
1 16-ounce package sauerkraut, drained
3 tablespoons brown sugar
1 onion, thinly sliced
½ teaspoon caraway seeds
2 bay leaves
1 can onion soup

Serves 4 to 6

Preheat the oven to 350°F. In a large skillet, lightly sauté the pork chops and apple in the butter, then remove to a casserole. Place the sauerkraut over the chops, sprinkle with the brown sugar, and top with the sliced onion. Add the caraway seeds, bay leaves, and onion soup. Cover and bake for 1 hour.

ROAST PORK
Arrosto di Maiale

Fennel seeds, a major flavoring ingredient in Italian sausages, permeate the pork as it slow roasts in the oven.

1 tablespoon dried rosemary
4 cloves garlic, minced
1 teaspoon fennel seeds
2 tablespoons olive oil
1 tablespoon fresh lemon juice
Freshly ground black pepper to taste
Salt to taste (optional)
4½ to 5 pounds boneless pork loin

Serves 6 to 8

Preheat the oven to 425°F. In a small bowl, mix the rosemary, garlic, fennel seeds, oil, lemon juice, pepper, and salt. Spread over the top and sides of the pork as far as it will go.

Place the pork in a roasting pan and tent with aluminum foil. Roast for 20 minutes, then reduce the oven temperature to 375°F and bake for an additional 1½ to 2 hours, or until the internal meat temperature is 180°F.

Remove from the oven and let rest for 20 minutes before carving.

SAUSAGES WITH BEANS
Salsicce e Fagioli

This quick, easy dish is lighter than the traditional version, but still delicious.

6 to 8 Italian sweet sausages
3 tablespoons olive oil
1½ cups fresh or canned plum tomatoes, chopped
Freshly ground black pepper to taste
Salt to taste (optional)
1 19-ounce can *cannellini* **(white kidney beans), drained**

Serves 4

Pierce or slit the sausages and place in a large skillet. Fill the skillet halfway with water and bring to a boil. When almost all the water has evaporated, pour off the residue.

Add the olive oil to the skillet and brown the sausages. Then add the tomatoes, pepper, and salt and simmer for 10 to 15 minutes. Add the beans and continue to simmer another 20 minutes. Serve.

FLORENTINE STEAK
Bistecca alla Fiorentina

A few years ago I enjoyed a very leisurely lunch in Florence, Italy, which stretched to about three and a half hours. Of course, this was research work, and although tedious, someone had to do it! People kept joining our table, which accounted for the many espressos and anisettes consumed. The lunch was exceptional and delectable. Florentine grilling is plain, simple, and enticing.

For all of you barbecue aficionados, here is the simplest of Florentine grilled beefs.

2 large porterhouse or T-bone steaks
1 tablespoon extra virgin olive oil
Freshly ground black pepper to taste
Salt to taste (optional)
2 lemons, cut into wedges

Serves 4 to 6

The grill should be hot, hot, hot! Brush the steaks with the olive oil and add pepper (do not salt before cooking).

Grill the steaks until medium-rare (an instant-reading thermometer is the answer to many cooking woes). Add salt if desired. Surround with lemon wedges.

SAUSAGES WITH LENTILS

Salsicce e Lenticchie

1 medium onion, chopped
2 cloves garlic, whole
1 stalk celery, chopped
3 tablespoons olive oil
2 quarts water
½ pound dried lentils (soaked overnight and drained)
½ teaspoon tomato paste
⅛ teaspoon crushed red pepper flakes
1 bay leaf
Freshly ground black pepper to taste
Salt to taste (optional)
6 to 8 Italian sweet sausages
Grated Parmesan cheese
2 tablespoons chopped fresh Italian parsley

Serves 4 to 6

In a large skillet, sauté the onion, garlic, and celery in 2 tablespoons of the olive oil until soft. Add the water, lentils, tomato paste, red pepper flakes, bay leaf, black pepper, and salt. Bring to boil, then reduce the heat to a simmer. Cook for about 1 hour.

Meanwhile, pierce or slit the sausages and place in another large skillet filled halfway with water; bring to a boil. When most of the water has evaporated, pour off the residue. Add the remaining tablespoon of olive oil to the skillet and brown the sausages.

Add the sausages to the lentils (after they have cooked 1 hour) and simmer for another 30 to 60 minutes. Discard the bay leaf before serving.

Sprinkle with Parmesan cheese and chopped parsley and serve.

AUNT IDA'S MEATBALLS WITH CAPERS

Polpettine ai Capperi della Zia Ida

Aunt Ida (Dad's only sister) had a thing about capers. So while Dad had Mom put raisins in our meatballs, Aunt Ida put in capers, and now I love them.
They do become addictive, so you may want to double the recipe.

½ pound lean ground beef
½ pound lean ground pork
½ teaspoon dried oregano
2 large eggs or 4 large egg whites, beaten
2 tablespoons grated Parmesan cheese
¾ cup fine bread crumbs
Freshly ground black pepper to taste
½ cup chopped fresh Italian parsley
1½ tablespoons drained small capers
Salt to taste (optional)
2 tablespoons olive oil for frying

Serves 4

Mix the meat with all the other ingredients *except* the olive oil. Form the mixture into approximately 8 meatballs.

Frying Method: Heat the oil in a large skillet and brown and cook the meatballs with the cover on.

Oven Method: Preheat the oven to 400°F and bake the meatballs for 20 minutes. Lower the oven temperature to 375°F and bake for an additional 30 to 40 minutes, or until the internal temperature of the meatballs is 180°F.

The meatballs can be served plain or in tomato sauce.

STUFFED PEPPERS ON RICE

Peperoni Ripieni su Riso

I must admit that for years I felt that stuffed peppers were far too boring for my consideration. But along came this Italian version, with its creamy rice filling—it is really full of flavor.

STUFFED PEPPERS
6 red bell peppers
½ medium onion, minced
1 tablespoon olive oil
12 ounces ground veal
8 ounces ground pork
1 tablespoon pine nuts
⅛ teaspoon grated nutmeg
1 teaspoon Dijon mustard
2 tablespoons heavy cream
2 tablespoons grated Romano cheese
Salt to taste (optional)
3 cups chicken broth (recipe on page 15)

RICE
1 cup Italian short-grain rice
¼ teaspoon ground dried rosemary
Freshly ground black pepper to taste
Salt to taste (optional)
1 cup peas
2 tablespoons unsalted butter
2 tablespoons grated Romano cheese

Serves 4 to 6

Cut the tops off the peppers and set aside. Remove the seeds and membranes.

In a medium skillet, sauté the onion in the olive oil until translucent. Add the meat and lightly brown.

Drain off any drippings and transfer the meat to a large bowl. Add the pine nuts, nutmeg, mustard, cream, Romano cheese, and salt and mix thoroughly.

Stuff the peppers with the meat mixture and place in a saucepan with 2 cups of the broth. Place the tops of the peppers on them and simmer, covered, for 35 to 40 minutes. Remove the peppers from the saucepan and wrap in foil to keep warm.

Add the rice to the broth remaining in the saucepan (there will be approximately 2 cups). Add the rosemary, pepper, and salt and bring to a boil. Add another cup of broth and simmer, stirring for about 20 minutes. When the rice is almost cooked, add the peas, butter, and cheese.

Place a pepper in the center of dinner plate and attractively arrange rice around it. Serve.

SICILIAN MEAT LOAF

Polpettone alla Siciliana

My Sicilian meat loaf will surprise your dinner guests—the secret is the cheese mixture that is baked right into the meat. A big hit with kids.

12 ounces lean ground beef
12 ounces lean ground pork
¾ cup bread crumbs
2 large eggs or 4 large egg whites, beaten
¼ cup grated caciocavallo or Romano cheese
½ teaspoon dried ground thyme
1 small onion, minced
¼ teaspoon grated nutmeg
1 cup marinara sauce (recipe on page 67)
Freshly ground black pepper to taste
Salt to taste (optional)
2 cups ricotta cheese
1 slice prosciutto, diced
6 plum tomatoes, chopped
1 tablespoon chopped fresh Italian parsley

Serves 4 to 6

(continued)

Preheat the oven to 350°F. Mix the meat with the bread crumbs, eggs, cheese, thyme, onion, nutmeg, tomato sauce, pepper, and salt.

Pack the mixture into a greased loaf pan measuring approximately 10 by 5¾ inches. With a knife, clear a trench approximately 2 inches deep by 2½ inches wide down the middle of the loaf, pushing the meat to the side (the trench will be filled later with the ricotta mixture). Bake for 1 hour.

Meanwhile, mix the ricotta with the prosciutto and set aside.

After 1 hour, remove the meat loaf from the oven and place the ricotta cheese mixture in the center of the trench. Top with the tomatoes, sprinkle with parsley, and bake for an additional 20 minutes, or until the meat is thoroughly cooked. Serve.

LAMB STEW
Stufato di Agnello

On winter weekdays at home, there was always a huge kettle of stew on the stove. Somehow, as Mom would say, "It took the chill out of the cold." In this version, I add the vegetables later in the cooking process so that they keep their identities when the stew is ready.

2 tablespoons olive oil
1 clove garlic, minced
2 pounds lamb shoulder or boneless lamb for stew, cut into 1-inch
  cubes
1 teaspoon dried rosemary
1 bay leaf
Freshly ground black pepper to taste
Salt to taste (optional)
2 cups water
1 cup beef stock
1 cup dry red wine
1 cup chopped plum tomatoes

4 carrots, peeled and cut into chunks
4 small whole onions, peeled and quartered
2 stalks celery, cut into pieces
2 medium potatoes, sliced but not peeled
1 cup peas
2 tablespoons all-purpose flour dissolved in 3 tablespoons water
2 tablespoons chopped fresh Italian parsley

Serves 6

In a large Dutch oven, heat the olive oil and add the garlic. Sauté the garlic for 1 minute, then add the meat and brown on all sides in the hot oil. Add the rosemary, bay leaf, pepper, salt, water, stock, and wine. Cover the pan and simmer 45 minutes to 1 hour, stirring occasionally.

Add the vegetables, cover, and cook 30 minutes longer, or until the meat and vegetables are tender.

Add the flour and water mixture to thicken the stew. Taste and add more seasonings if desired. Remove the bay leaf and sprinkle with the parsley.

ROAST LEG OF LAMB

Agnello Arrosto

This recipe has been the hit of many family barbecues. The fragrant filling permeates the succulent meat. It's just as delicious when oven-roasted, as is done here.

1 boned leg of lamb (4–4½ pounds), butterflied
3 tablespoons olive oil
4 to 6 ounces fresh spinach
1 onion, chopped
1 tablespoon unsalted butter
4 ounces prosciutto, chopped
5 tablespoons bread crumbs
Pinch dried rosemary
¼ teaspoon freshly grated nutmeg
Freshly ground black pepper to taste
½ cup red wine
3 tablespoons grated Parmesan cheese

Serves 12 to 14 (one 3-ounce slice each)

Preheat the oven to 350°F. Pound the lamb to flatten it as evenly as possible into a rectangular piece. Brush the top with 1 tablespoon of the olive oil.

Steam the spinach in a covered saucepan, drain well, and finely chop.

In a large skillet, sauté the onion in the butter until translucent. Add the spinach, the remaining 2 tablespoons of olive oil, the prosciutto, bread crumbs, rosemary, nutmeg, and pepper. Cook for 3 to 4 minutes. Add the wine and simmer over medium heat until all the liquid is absorbed.

Spread the filling over the entire surface of the lamb. Sprinkle the grated cheese over the filling. Carefully roll the meat, jelly roll fashion, and tie it in several places.

Place in a roasting pan and roast for 1¼ to 1¾ hours for rare, or longer to desired doneness.

LIVER VENETIAN STYLE

Fegato alla Veneziana

I've added a modest amount of salt to this recipe. I feel that it's necessary to complement the sautéed onions, and without the onions, the dish isn't Venetian.

2 large onions, thinly sliced
2 tablespoons unsalted butter
3 tablespoons olive oil
1½ pounds calf's liver, very thinly sliced
¼ teaspoon salt
Freshly ground black pepper to taste
½ cup chopped fresh Italian parsley

Serves 4

In a large skillet, sauté the onions in the butter and oil until translucent. Add the liver and sauté briskly on both sides to your liking. Add the salt and pepper and sprinkle with parsley. Serve immediately.

Sweet and Sour Calf's Liver
Fegato "Garbo e Dolce"

Despite the fact that, as a child, I was repeatedly told, "Eat your liver; it's good for you," I really did eat my liver and I even learned to love it—especially when my mother cooked it sweet and sour style. She taught me that the success of the dish is in the selection of only the freshest, thinnest cuts of calf's liver—and the sugar and lemon help!

1¼ to 1½ pounds calf's liver, cut into thin strips
½ cup all-purpose flour
3 large egg whites, beaten
1 cup fine bread crumbs
¼ cup (½ stick) unsalted butter
¼ cup olive oil
Juice of 2 lemons
1 tablespoon sugar
1 tablespoon chopped fresh Italian parsley

Serves 4

Dredge the liver in the flour, dip in the egg whites, then press into the bread crumbs to coat.

Heat the butter and oil in a medium skillet. Add the liver and brown on both sides; remove from the skillet to a plate and cover to keep warm.

Using the same skillet, heat the lemon juice and sugar, then pour over the liver. Sprinkle with parsley and serve.

CHAPTER 8

❧

Poultry
Pollame

Sometimes I think that America is in danger of turning into one giant chicken McNugget! Today's dietary concerns have prompted people to constantly ask me for yet another new chicken recipe. Everytime I cook chicken on TV, the recipe requests are their heaviest.

Luckily, viewers have come to the right place. In the American Italian kitchen, chicken never has a chance to be boring. Just for starters, check out my chicken with artichokes, my simple flavor-infused herb-roasted chicken, and Aunt Mary's zippy Sicilian chicken.

And although not as popular as chicken with the general population, my duck and turkey recipes get rave reviews with family and friends. My favorites are the top-of-stove-prepared Ligurian duck and turkey marsala. I also encourage you to think of recipes that call for turkey or chicken cutlets as interchangeable.

SICILIAN CHICKEN

Pollo alla Siciliana

Aunt Mary would fix this dish and tell me, "Eat! Eat!" She was married to a Sicilian who made it a rule to eat only fish and chicken fixed this way.

Many old recipes call for stirring fat drippings into the sauce. I don't recommend that you eat rendered fat, but I've duplicated the taste with a base of garlic, celery, and olives married with stock, tomato paste, and a little vermouth.

1 3 to 4-pound chicken, cut into 12 pieces
3 tablespoons olive oil
¼ cup white vermouth
2 cloves garlic
2 tablespoons drained small capers
2 stalks celery, chopped
2 bay leaves
1 tablespoon tomato paste
1 cup chicken broth (recipe on page 15)
1 tablespoon dried thyme
¼ teaspoon crushed red pepper flakes
Freshly ground black pepper to taste
Salt to taste (optional)
1 cup pitted and sliced green olives

Serves 4

In a large skillet, brown the chicken in 1 tablespoon of the oil. When all the pieces are nicely browned, remove from the skillet and discard any rendered fat.

Add the vermouth, remaining olive oil, garlic, capers, celery, and bay leaves to the skillet. When the celery is soft, mix the tomato paste with the stock and stir in. Add the thyme, red pepper flakes, black pepper, salt, and olives. Return the chicken to the skillet and simmer, covered, for 40 minutes.

Uncover and simmer an additional 20 minutes, or until the chicken is cooked. Remove the bay leaves.

If the sauce has not reduced to ⅔, remove the chicken and reduce the sauce over high heat; pour over the chicken and serve.

ROAST CHICKEN WITH WALNUT STUFFING

Pollo Arroste con Ripieno di Noci

The ingredients may sound festive enough for a holiday meal, but this roast chicken is wonderful any night of the week.

1 4-pound roasting chicken
1 small onion, chopped
1 stalk celery, chopped
1 cup chopped walnuts
8 dried prunes, pitted and chopped
1 apple, peeled and diced
2 tablespoons unsalted butter
2 tablespoons olive oil
1 pound ground veal
½ cup brandy
½ teaspoon poultry seasoning
¼ teaspoon white pepper
¼ teaspoon ground allspice
⅛ teaspoon grated nutmeg
¼ cup grated Parmesan cheese
2 large egg whites, beaten

Serves 4 to 6

Preheat the oven to 375°F. Clean and prepare the chicken for roasting.

In a large skillet, sauté the onion, celery, walnuts, prunes, and apple in the butter and olive oil. When the vegetables are soft, add the veal and brandy and cook lightly.

Transfer the mixture to a bowl and mix in the poultry seasoning, pepper, allspice, nutmeg, cheese, and egg whites.

Stuff the seasoned mixture into the chicken and truss or skewer. Any remaining stuffing can be enclosed in a foil packet and baked alongside the chicken. Roast the chicken for 1 hour, then lower the oven temperature to 350°F and roast another hour, or until completely cooked.

CHICKEN CUTLETS
Cotolette di Pollo

8 chicken cutlets, sliced thin
1 large egg, lightly beaten
¼ cup milk
2 tablespoons grated Parmesan cheese
1 tablespoon chopped fresh Italian parsley
⅛ teaspoon white pepper
Salt to taste (optional)
1 cup bread crumbs
3 tablespoons olive oil

Serves 4

Pound the cutlets thin. In a shallow bowl, mix the egg, milk, cheese, parsley, pepper, and salt. Dip the cutlets into the mixture, then press into the bread crumbs.

In a large skillet, sauté the cutlets in the olive oil until golden brown and cooked.

Chicken in White Wine and Tomato Sauce

Spezzatino di Pollo

This dish can be as elegant or economical as you wish, depending on the poultry parts you choose. Use only chicken breasts or substitute duck—whatever tempts you.

1 3 to 4-pound chicken, cut into 12 pieces
2 tablespoons olive oil
¾ cup dry white wine
2 tablespoons unsalted butter
1 teaspoon dried rosemary
Freshly ground black pepper to taste
Salt to taste (optional)
1 cup marinara sauce (recipe on page 67)
4 ounces mushrooms, sliced

Serves 4

In a large skillet, brown the chicken in 1 tablespoon of the olive oil. When all pieces are nicely browned, discard any rendered fat.

Add the wine, butter, remaining oil, rosemary, pepper, and salt to the skillet. Cover and let simmer for 25 to 30 minutes. Add the tomato sauce and mushrooms and continue to simmer, uncovered, for an additional 30 minutes, until the chicken is cooked.

If the sauce has not reduced one quarter, remove the chicken and reduce the sauce over high heat; pour over the chicken and serve.

CREAMED CHICKEN AND NOODLES

Pollo Tetrazzini

Creamed dishes are a favorite of young and old alike, but nowadays many people prefer leaner versions. My pollo tetrazzini *should satisfy both our taste buds and our arteries.*

By the way, this is a great way to use leftover chicken. Turkey may be used as a substitute.

8 ounces fettuccine or eggless noodles
1 cup sliced mushrooms
3 tablespoons unsalted butter or margarine
2 tablespoons all-purpose flour
1¼ cups 1% low-fat milk
1 cup chicken broth (recipe on page 15)
⅛ teaspoon grated nutmeg
⅛ teaspoon white pepper
⅛ teaspoon sweet paprika
1 large egg, beaten
¼ cup grated Parmesan cheese
1 cup baby peas
2 cups cooked chicken in bite-size pieces
Salt to taste (optional)
Italian parsley sprigs, for garnish

Serves 4

Cook the pasta in the usual way (see page 47).

Meanwhile, in a skillet, sauté the mushrooms in the butter; add the flour and mix into a roux. Cook the roux slowly until golden, then add the milk and broth and blend together. Mix in the nutmeg, pepper, and paprika, blend in the egg and cheese. Mix well, then add the peas, cooked chicken, and salt. Simmer and stir for several minutes, until thick and creamy.

Drain the pasta well and dress with the cream sauce and garnish with parsley.

CHICKEN HUNTER STYLE
Pollo alla Cacciatora

1 3 to 4-pound chicken, cut into 12 pieces
3 tablespoons olive oil
2 cloves garlic
2 small onions, chopped
1 stalk celery, chopped
8 ripe plum tomatoes (or 1 20-ounce can), chopped
2 bay leaves
½ tablespoon dried sage
1 tablespoon dried rosemary
Freshly ground black pepper to taste
Salt to taste (optional)
1½ cups chicken broth (recipe on page 15)
¾ cup dry red wine
4 ounces whole button mushrooms
¾ cup long-grain rice

Serves 4

In a large skillet, brown the chicken in 1 tablespoon of the olive oil. When all the pieces are browned, remove the chicken from the skillet. Discard any rendered fat.

In the same skillet, sauté the garlic, onions, and celery in the remaining 2 tablespoons of olive oil until soft; add the tomatoes, bay leaves, sage, rosemary, pepper, and salt. Return the chicken to the skillet, cover, and simmer for 25 to 30 minutes. Add the broth, wine, and mushrooms, and scatter the rice over all the ingredients. Continue to simmer, uncovered, for an additional 30 minutes, until the chicken and rice are cooked.

ROASTED CHICKEN WITH LEMON

Pollo Arrosto al Limone

Simplicity is the secret to great-tasting chicken in the following two recipes. The first is infused with tangy lemon and pungent garlic and the second with the aromatic flavor of basil. Both use skinless chicken and so are lower in fat.

1 3–3½-pound chicken, skinless
Freshly ground black pepper to taste
Salt to taste (optional)
2 lemons, quartered
4 cloves garlic, crushed
Juice of 2 lemons
2 tablespoons grated lemon zest
3 tablespoons olive oil
1 lemon, cut into wedges
Sprigs fresh Italian parsley, for garnish

Serves 4

Preheat the oven to 375°F. Clean and prepare the chicken for roasting. Place the pepper, salt, quartered lemons, and garlic in the cavity of the chicken.

In a small bowl, mix the lemon juice and zest with the olive oil. Brush half of the mixture on the chicken and roast in oven pan for 40 minutes. Then brush the remaining mixture on the chicken and roast an additional 40 minutes, or until cooked.

Cut into serving pieces and serve with lemon wedges. Garnish with parsley sprigs.

CHICKEN WITH FENNEL

Pollo al Finocchio

This is an easy, healthful dish that uses no oil or butter in cooking. If your family has become bored with chicken dishes, the fennel will provide them with a fresh, unexpected taste.

2 medium to large chicken breasts, cut in half and boned
1 medium onion, minced
2 cloves garlic
Juice of ½ lemon
Salt to taste (optional)
Freshly ground black pepper to taste
1 teaspoon fennel seeds

Serves 4

Place the chicken breast halves in a large nonstick skillet, skin side down, and brown them quickly. Reduce the heat and add the onion and garlic. Cover and cook for 15 to 20 minutes.

Remove the chicken from the skillet and discard any fat. Return the chicken to the skillet and add the lemon juice, salt, pepper, and fennel seeds. Cover and cook until the chicken is done, approximately 15 minutes.

ROASTED CHICKEN WITH BASIL

Pollo Arrosto al Basile

1 3 to 3½-pound chicken, skinless
Freshly ground black pepper to taste
Salt to taste (optional)
4 cloves garlic, crushed
Several sprigs fresh basil
3 tablespoons olive oil
1 lemon, cut into wedges

Serves 4

Preheat the oven to 375°F. Clean and prepare the chicken for roasting. Place the pepper, salt, garlic, and a few sprigs of basil in the cavity of the chicken.

Chop the rest of the basil and mix with the olive oil in a small bowl. Brush half of the mixture on the chicken and roast for 40 minutes. Brush the remaining mixture on the chicken and roast for an additional 40 minutes, or until cooked.

Cut into serving pieces and serve with lemon wedges.

CHICKEN WITH ARTICHOKES

Pollo ai Carciofi

Here is the baby artichoke at its best! First it is given a quick sauté in olive oil, then it is slow-simmered in wine and finally joined with golden chicken chunks and sprinkled with cheese.

2 large whole chicken breasts (1½ pounds each), skinned and boned
All-purpose flour, approximately ¼ cup (or more if needed)
3 tablespoons olive oil
8 small (baby) artichokes, trimmed of tough outer leaves and cut up
½ cup white wine
Freshly ground black pepper to taste
Salt to taste (optional)
2 tablespoons grated Parmesan cheese

Serves 4

Cut the chicken into chunks and dust with the flour. In a large skillet, sauté the chicken in the olive oil. Remove when cooked and set aside.

In the same skillet, sauté the artichoke pieces until soft. Add the wine, pepper, and salt and simmer, covered, for 15 minutes. Then add the chicken and simmer, uncovered, for 5 to 8 minutes.

Remove from the heat, sprinkle with cheese, and serve.

LIGURIAN SAUTÉED DUCKLINGS

Anatra in Padella all Ligure

This recipe, which comes from the Italian region of Liguria, where some of the most delicious olives are grown, is easily prepared on top of the stove. The juices and flavors are subtle, yet bold enough for the strong-flavored duck. If you don't want to cut the duckling up yourself, ask your butcher to do it.

2 large ducklings, about 4 pounds each
2 tablespoons olive oil
2 tablespoons unsalted butter
1 medium onion, finely chopped
1 carrot, finely chopped
1 cup dry white wine
2 bay leaves
2 tablespoons chopped fresh Italian parsley
¾ teaspoon dried thyme
Freshly ground black pepper to taste
Salt to taste (optional)
30 to 36 green olives, pitted and sliced
1 cup chicken broth (recipe on page 15)
½ pound mushrooms, sliced
Watercress, for garnish

Serves 6 to 8

If you're using frozen ducklings, defrost them in the refrigerator overnight. Use a large, heavy knife to cut each duckling in half lengthwise through the breastbone and backbone. Cut the legs from the body, and separate the drumsticks from the thighs. Cut off the wings and discard them. Cut the breast halves across into 2 pieces, cutting off and discarding the attached backbone. You will now have 8 pieces from each duckling.

Cut away any excess fat. Wash the pieces and pat them dry.

Place 8 pieces of duckling in a large skillet, skin side down. Cover and cook over low heat without any oil for 15 to 20 minutes. Remove the duckling and discard the rendered fat. Repeat with the other 8 pieces. Remove the duckling and discard the fat.

In the same skillet, heat the oil and butter and sauté the onion and carrot for about 3 minutes.

Add the wine and scrape the bottom of the skillet to loosen the little browned bits. Return the browned duckling pieces to the skillet and add the bay leaves, parsley, thyme, pepper, salt, olives, and broth. Cover and cook for 20 to 30 minutes.

Add the mushrooms to the skillet and check the seasonings. You may add another ½ teaspoon thyme or more pepper and salt. Continue cooking for approximately another 20 minutes, until the duckling is completely cooked—that is, when you prick it with a fork, the juices run clear, not pink. Remove the bay leaves before serving. Tuck the watercress between pieces of duck as a garnish.

TURKEY CUTLETS WITH MARSALA SAUCE

Petti di Tacchino al Marsala

I was cooking with versatile, economical turkey cutlets years before they became a supermarket staple. This particular dish works equally well with veal, chicken, or even pork cutlets. What makes it special is the Sicilian marsala, which has a hint of burned sugar that blends well with the butter.

4 large turkey cutlets
All-purpose flour, approximately ¼ cup (or more if needed)
1 tablespoon olive oil
3 tablespoons unsalted butter
¾ cup dry marsala
¼ teaspoon white pepper
Salt to taste (optional)
⅛ teaspoon grated nutmeg

Serves 4

Pound the cutlets thin and dust lightly with the flour. In a medium skillet, gently sauté the cutlets in the olive oil and butter until cooked. Remove to a warm platter.

Add the marsala, pepper, salt, and nutmeg to the skillet. Cook over high heat, stirring constantly, until thickened. Remove from the heat.

Return the turkey cutlets to the skillet to bathe in the sauce. Serve.

CHAPTER 9

❧

Desserts
Dolci

*A*t our family's dinner table, a bowl of fruit was dessert most of the time. Sweets were usually reserved for special occasions. (Talk about being in vogue with healthful trends!)

Mom would always bake mouth-watering traditional *dolci* for company and holiday dinners, especially at Easter, when we had chocolate candies, cookies, and her cheesecake. There were special pastries for each saint's day—cookies of San Martino on horseback for his feast day in November and a doughnut-type pastry for San Giuseppe's day in March. San Giuseppe (Saint Joseph) is not only the patron saint of the family but also the patron of pastry chefs.

In an Italian family, enough is never enough for guests, and even though Mom had baked up a storm, my brother and I would be sent off to the pastry shop to buy more assorted pastries. "Holy *cannoli,*" we would tease Mom. "Big shots" was always her reply. All the guests took home "doggie bags" and still our family would wind up with a month's supply of desserts.

Sometimes Mom would bake something special for our TV snack. We were allowed to watch only after homework was done, and since I was older, I had to tutor my brother. Our sessions often got loud, even messy. After the last spitball was fired and the last pencil broken, Mom and Dad would have to sign our homework. Believe me, I *earned* my piece of cake.

Some nights I would experiment and try one of those "new" boxed cake mixes or frozen dough things. But early on, I realized that for soul-satisfying sweets, you had to make them from scratch.

One of my earliest dates was a baking date in the fourth grade. I invited a girl from my class over to the house to make brownies with me. I don't think that the brownies turned out so great, but the pleasure of learning to bake as a child stayed with me, and when I developed my Little Chefs cooking program, I combined that sense of play and learning in my classes.

To me, *dolci* are always a celebration.

CHOCOLATE RICOTTA PUDDING
Budino di Ricotta e Cioccolata

15 ounces low-fat ricotta cheese
½ cup confectioners' sugar
1½ tablespoons unsweetened cocoa
1 square semisweet chocolate, grated
1 teaspoon vanilla extract
4–6 slices chocolate chip pound cake

Serves 4 to 6

Force the ricotta through a sieve or strainer over a bowl. Sift in the confectioners' sugar and add the cocoa, grated chocolate, and vanilla; cream together.

If desired, use with chocolate raspberry sauce (page 187).

Spoon some sauce on a small dessert plate and swirl from the center to cover three-quarters of the plate. Place the pound cake in the center and spoon chocolate cream on top.

CHOCOLATE RASPBERRY SAUCE

Salsa di Cioccolata e Lamponi

Almost everyone seems to love the blending of rich chocolate and raspberry. I like to serve this sauce with fresh raspberries all around.

¼ cup raspberry jam
1 tablespoon unsweetened cocoa
1 tablespoon cornstarch
½ cup water

Serves 4 to 6

In a small saucepan, mix the jam and cocoa and set over low heat. Mix the cornstarch with the water, add to the mixture, and simmer, stirring, until it is thick and smooth. Let cool.

POACHED PEARS WITH RASPBERRY SAUCE
Pere Affrogate con Salsa di Lamponi

Mother Nature gave us the basics for this dessert, and I just guided her hand.

6 cups water
¾ cup sugar
1 tablespoon grenadine syrup
1 tablespoon grated lemon zest
1 tablespoon vanilla extract
4 whole cloves
1 cinnamon stick
6 pears
1 tablespoon lemon juice
1 10-ounce package frozen raspberries, thawed
½ cup raspberry preserves
1 tablespoon cornstarch
Whipped cream (optional)

Serves 6

In a large saucepan, mix the water, sugar, grenadine, lemon zest, vanilla, cloves, and cinnamon stick; bring to a boil.

Meanwhile, core the pears from the bottom; also cut a thin slice off the bottom so the pears can stand upright. Peel and leave stems intact. Place the pears in the boiling liquid and simmer 20 to 30 minutes.

Remove the pears, brush on lemon juice to prevent discoloring, and chill. Reserve ½ cup of the cooking liquid.

In a saucepan, combine the raspberries, and preserves. Dissolve the cornstarch in the reserved pear liquid and stir into the raspberry mixture. Simmer until the mixture thickens.

Arrange each pear in a pool of raspberry sauce and top with whipped cream if desired.

CORNMEAL CAKES
Torta di Polenta

I like to offer generous slices of this cake with a mixture of fresh strawberries and blueberries and a dollop of whipped cream flavored with brandy.

1 cup all-purpose flour
½ cup yellow cornmeal
1 teaspoon baking powder
1 teaspoon grated lemon zest
½ cup chopped toasted almonds
1 large egg
3 large egg whites
½ cup sugar
½ cup applesauce
1 teaspoon almond extract

Serves 8 to 10

Preheat the oven to 350°F. In a large bowl, combine the flour, cornmeal, and baking powder; add the lemon zest and almonds.

In another bowl, beat the egg and egg whites, add the sugar, and beat, beat, beat. Add the applesauce and almond extract and beat again.

Now fold this mixture into the flour mixture.

Grease and flour a 9-inch springform pan. Add the mixture and bake for approximately 30 minutes or until done.

CENCI

"Fried Knots" is the literal translation of these traditional pastries.

2 cups all-purpose flour
1 teaspoon baking powder
1½ teaspoons sugar
⅛ teaspoon salt
2 tablespoons unsalted butter
2 large eggs
1 tablespoon brandy
1 tablespoon vanilla extract
Oil or shortening for deep-frying (use extra light olive oil if you wish)
Confectioners' sugar for sprinkling

Serves 4

Sift the flour into a large bowl together with the baking powder, sugar, and salt. Cut in the butter.

In a separate bowl, lightly beat the eggs with the brandy and vanilla. Add this to the flour mixture and mix together into a workable dough. Knead and let rest in a cool place for about 1 hour, covered with a cloth.

Divide the dough into four workable pieces and very thinly roll each out paper thin on a floured surface. Cut into strips 5½ to 6 inches long and about 1 inch wide.

Deep-fry the knots, a few at a time, in very hot oil (400°F) until they are golden tan. Drain on paper towels.

When cool, arrange the knots in a high mound, sprinkle with confectioners' sugar, and serve with ice cream, sherbet, or fruit. They are also delicious all by themselves!

STUFFED PEACHES

Pesche Ripiene

A light and elegant summer treat.

1½ tablespoons sugar
2 tablespoons unsalted butter, melted
6 amaretti, crumbled
½ teaspoon ground cinnamon
2 tablespoons pine nuts
2 large egg whites, beaten
8 peach halves, fresh peeled or canned

Serves 4

Preheat the oven to 375°F. In a large bowl, mix the sugar, melted butter, amaretti, cinnamon, and pine nuts, then fold in the egg whites that have been beaten to soft peaks.

Fill the peach cavities with the mixture, piling it high in the center. Bake for 40 minutes.

PEACHES WITH WINE

Pesche al Vino

Watching adults enjoy this simplest of after-dinner delights makes me realize that "grown-up" desserts can be just as much fun as the sweet-sweet ice creams and cakes that children love.

4 fresh ripe peaches
1 teaspoon sugar
1 teaspoon fresh lemon juice
1 cup red wine

Serves 4

(continued)

Peel, pit, and cut the peaches into bite-size pieces. Sprinkle with sugar. Add the lemon juice and wine. Refrigerate before serving.

Variation: Substitute pears for peaches.

CREAM PUFF PASTRY
Pasta Reale

Fill with your favorite custard or use chocolate cannoli cream (page 200). Pipe the filling into the shells with a pastry bag or slice the shells in half and fill. Serve with a dusting of confectioners' sugar.

1 cup water
½ cup (1 stick) unsalted butter
Pinch salt
1 cup all-purpose flour
4 large eggs, beaten
Confectioners' sugar for dusting

Yields approximately 3 dozen puffs

Preheat the oven to 425°F. Bring the water to a boil in a medium saucepan and melt the butter in it. Add the salt. Dump in the flour all at once, stirring briskly with a wooden spoon. When it is well mixed, remove the pan from the heat and slowly beat in the eggs until well blended.

Drop by tablespoons onto a greased baking sheet, being careful not to place the dough mounds too close together. (Lightly greasing the spoon keeps the dough from sticking.)

Bake the puffs for about 18 minutes, then lower the oven temperature to 350°F and cook about 10 minutes more. The puffs should be golden brown. You can make the puffs up to 8 hours in advance; store in a dry place.

TIRAMISÙ

This is indeed a "pick-me-up" (the literal translation of its name), with its rich ingredients. It features imported Italian mascarpone cheese. This creamy cheese, which is now more readily available nationwide, tastes somewhat like cream cheese but is sweeter. This recipe features pound cake instead of the traditional ladyfingers or sponge cake.

1 cup whipping cream
1 pound mascarpone cheese
¾ cup confectioners' sugar
3 tablespoons amaretto liqueur
1 teaspoon vanilla extract
3 ounces brewed strong espresso, cooled
1 loaf pound cake, plain or chocolate chip, approximately 7½ by 3½ inches
Unsweetened cocoa powder
Chocolate shavings, for garnish (optional)

Serves 6 to 8

In a medium bowl, whip the cream into soft peaks and set aside.

In a large bowl, cream the mascarpone cheese with the sugar, then fold in the whipped cream.

Add the amaretto and vanilla to the cooled espresso.

Carefully cut two 1-inch-thick slices from the pound cake *horizontally* (there will be cake left over). Place the bottom cake slice on a large serving platter, drizzle or brush on half of the espresso mixture, then spoon on half of the cheese mixture. Top with the other slice of cake, pressing down slightly; brush on the rest of the espresso and top with the remaining cheese mixture. Dust the top with cocoa powder (use a small tea strainer) and garnish with chocolate shavings if desired.

MOM'S TRADITIONAL CHEESECAKE "REDESIGNED"

Torta di Ricotta della Mamma

After many a large family feast, when the sweets came out, everyone would say, "You've got to be kidding" (almost in unison).

We had no room left to eat another morsel, much less Mom's cheesecake, in which each slice had to weigh at least a pound. Even though it was quite delicious, it always seemed too heavy to eat after a huge meal.

Well, in all deference to Mom, here it is, lighter, fluffier, and, I think, just as delicious!

7 large egg whites
1½ pounds low-fat ricotta cheese
2 large egg yolks
1 cup sugar
Juice of ½ orange
1½ tablespoons vanilla extract
1 tablespoon anisette liqueur
1 teaspoon grated orange zest
1 teaspoon baking powder
Confectioners' sugar for sprinkling

Serves 8 to 12

Preheat the oven to 350°F. In a large bowl, beat the egg whites until stiff and set aside.

In a separate large bowl, mix the ricotta cheese with the egg yolks, sugar, orange juice, vanilla, anisette, orange zest, and baking powder. Fold in the egg whites.

Pour into a greased and floured 8-inch springform pan. Bake for 50 minutes to 1 hour. Check with a cake tester or toothpick inserted in the center of the cake. The tester should come out clean. When cooling, a little liquid may ooze out; this is normal. Sprinkle with confectioners' sugar and serve.

PUMPKIN CHEESECAKE
Torta di Ricotta e Zucca

Pumpkin and cheese is an unlikely combination that works beautifully.

7 large egg whites
1½ pounds ricotta cheese
2 large egg yolks
1 cup sugar
1½ cups puréed canned pumpkin
1½ tablespoons vanilla extract
1½ teaspoons pumpkin pie spice
1 teaspoon baking powder
Confectioners' sugar for sprinkling

Serves 8 to 12

Preheat the oven to 350°F. In a large bowl, beat the egg whites until stiff and set aside.

In a separate large bowl, mix the ricotta cheese with the egg yolks, sugar, pumpkin, vanilla, pumpkin pie spice, and baking powder. Fold in the egg whites.

Pour into a greased and floured 8-inch springform pan. Bake for 50 minutes to 1 hour. Check with a cake tester or toothpick inserted in the center of the cake. The tester should come out clean. The texture will resemble a soufflé. Let cool and refrigerate overnight. Dust with confectioners' sugar when serving.

PEARS BAKED WITH NUTS

Pere al Forno con Noci

Here's an easy dessert that can be dressed up for elegant occasions or kept simple for everyday meals.

4 pears, peeled, cored, and quartered
¼ cup light brown sugar
⅓ cup all-purpose flour
⅛ teaspoon pumpkin pie spice
3 tablespoons cold unsalted butter
¼ cup pine nuts or sliced almonds

Serves 4

Preheat the oven to 350°F. Grease a pie plate or similar baking dish, and scatter the pears in it.

In a small bowl, mix the sugar, flour, and pumpkin pie spice. Cut in the butter, then add the nuts.

Sprinkle over the pears and bake for 20 to 30 minutes, until the topping is golden brown.

Serve with freshly whipped cream—perhaps sweetened with brandy—or a premium vanilla ice cream.

SWEET FRIED PASTRIES

Zeppole

Walk through a festival in any Italian neighborhood in the United States, and you can find these fried delectables. But watch out, you almost need a bib to catch the confectioners' sugar!

2 cups all-purpose flour
⅛ teaspoon salt
½ cup sugar
3 teaspoons baking powder
¼ teaspoon ground allspice
2 large eggs, beaten
½ cup 1% low-fat milk
Shortening or oil for frying
Confectioners' sugar for sprinkling (optional)

Yields 20 to 30 pieces

In a large bowl, sift together the flour, salt, sugar, baking powder, and allspice. Add the eggs to the flour mixture together with the milk. Mix into a workable dough.

Let rest for about 30 minutes, covered with a cloth.

Heat the oil (375°F) in a deep-fryer until hot. Drop tablespoons of the dough into the oil, a few at a time. (Lightly greasing the spoon keeps the dough from sticking.) Deep-fry until golden brown, then drain on paper towels.

Sprinkle with confectioners' sugar before serving.

EGG CUSTARD
Zabaione

This Italian classic is from the Piedmont region. It's very rich, so small servings are suggested.

5 large egg yolks
5 teaspoons sugar
1 teaspoon grated orange zest
½ cup sweet marsala

Serves 4

(continued)

Beat the egg yolks, sugar, and orange zest together in the top of a double boiler and set over simmering water. Use a whisk and continue to beat, gradually adding the marsala.

Continue to beat until the mixture becomes foamy and thick. Serve warm or chilled.

Variation I: Sweeten and beat 1 cup heavy cream (or use ready-made dessert topping) and fold into the completed *zabaione*. Refrigerate for a few hours or freeze for 20 to 30 minutes before serving.

Variation II: Same as Variation I, except add 8 crumbled *amaretti* cookies to the mixture.

PEAR EGG CUSTARD
Pere alle Zabaione

This isn't just for company; it's a soul-satisfying treat anytime.

5 large egg yolks
5 teaspoons sugar
¼ teaspoon ground allspice
½ cup fruity pear schnapps or liqueur
2 ripe pears, peeled, cored, and halved
2 tablespoons pine nuts or almonds, sliced

Serves 4

Beat the egg yolks, sugar, and allspice together in the top of a double boiler and set over simmering water. Use a whisk and continue to beat. Gradually add the schnapps or liqueur and continue to beat until the mixture becomes foamy and thick.

Refrigerate for a few hours or freeze for 20 to 30 minutes before serving.

Set a pear half in each serving dish and spoon on the *zabaione*. Sprinkle with nuts.

STRUFFOLI

For special holidays like Christmas and Easter, struffoli *were always made one or two days in advance.*

These mounds of marble-sized fried honey dough balls with colored confetti were fun to eat, but the longer they were left, the harder they became.

4 cups all-purpose flour
⅔ cup sugar
4 tablespoons baking powder
2 large egg whites
4 large eggs
1 tablespoon vanilla extract
¼ cup (½ stick) unsalted butter, cut into small pieces
Pinch salt
½ cup oil or applesauce
Oil for deep-frying
1 cup honey
Candied confetti for sprinkling

Yields 5 to 6 dozen small balls

In a large bowl, combine the flour, sugar, and baking powder.

In another bowl, beat the egg whites until stiff. In a third bowl, beat the whole eggs with the vanilla, then fold into the egg whites. Now mix all the ingredients into the flour mixture, add the butter, salt, and oil or applesauce, and mix until well blended. Blend thoroughly into a dough and knead, then cover with a cloth and let rest for approximately 1 hour.

Cut or pull away the smaller pieces and roll them into cigar shapes. Then cut into small pieces and roughly roll into small marble-sized balls measuring about ½ inch.

Deep-fry in hot oil at 385°F until lightly browned and cooked through. Drain on paper towels.

Meanwhile, in a small saucepan, heat the honey until it is foamy. Plunge the *struffoli* into the honey quickly and remove to large plate. Arrange in a pyramid. Sprinkle with candied confetti.

CANNOLI

These pastries are at their best when eaten fresh!

If you buy them in a pastry shop, the shells should be filled only when you order them so they are crisp and crunchy when you bite into that creamy, satiny filling. A great sensation.

Italian bakers are always creative with their additions to the filling. Join the tradition!

FILLING
1 pound low-fat ricotta cheese
½ cup confectioners' sugar
1 tablespoon vanilla extract
1 tablespoon minced candied fruits
1 tablespoon chocolate jimmies, for garnish
½ cup finely chopped nuts, for garnish
Confectioners' sugar for sprinkling (optional)

SHELLS
1 cup all-purpose flour
1 tablespoon margarine or applesauce
Pinch salt
½ cup sweet marsala
Oil for deep-frying

Yields 8

Mix the ricotta cheese with the sugar, vanilla extract, and candied fruits; blend thoroughly. Reserve the jimmies and nuts for garnish. Refrigerate while making the shells.

Combine the flour with the margarine (or applesauce) and salt, then gradually add the marsala. Work into a dough and knead into a ball. Let rest for 15 to 20 minutes. Then divide in half and roll each half into a very thin sheet. Cut into 4-inch squares. You must have *cannoli* tubes (which are sold in specialty stores) for deep-frying the pastry. Place a tube in the center of a square, leaving a point on each end. Wrap around the tube overlapping the dough and seal the dough where touching. Deep-fry at 385°F until golden brown.

Remove and let cool, then carefully slide the shell off the tube. When ready to serve, fill each shell, then dip one end in jimmies and the other in nuts.

Lightly sprinkle with confectioners' sugar if desired, then serve.

LOW-FAT APPLE PANCAKES
Frittelle di Mele

Good at breakfast or brunch and as a dessert or midnight snack.

2 apples, peeled, cored, and thinly sliced
1 cup pancake mix
1 cup skim milk
2 large egg whites
2 tablespoons applesauce
½ teaspoon pumpkin pie spice
1 teaspoon vanilla extract
½ cup sliced almonds

Yields 4 large pancakes

In a medium bowl, combine the apples with the pancake mix. In a separate bowl, mix the milk, egg whites, applesauce, pumpkin pie spice, and vanilla, then stir into the pancake mix.

Coat a griddle with cooking spray, then heat. Pour one-quarter of the batter on the hot griddle. When the batter begins to bubble, sprinkle with some nuts, turn, and cook until second side is browned.

Repeat with the remaining batter.

PINE NUT COOKIES

Biscotti con Pignoli

1 whole large egg
3 large egg whites
⅔ cup sugar
½ tablespoon almond paste
1 cup all-purpose flour
1 teaspoon orange juice
½ teaspoon almond extract
½ teaspoon vanilla extract
2–3 ounces pine nuts

Yields approximately 2 dozen cookies

Preheat the oven to 375°F.

In the top of a double boiler, mix the egg, egg whites, sugar, and almond paste. Set over simmering water and whisk until the mixture is smooth.

Remove from the heat and whisk until cooled, then beat in the flour, a little at a time.

Finally, incorporate the orange juice and both of the extracts.

Grease and flour a baking sheet and place teaspoons of the dough, well spaced, on it. Let the dough rest on the baking sheet for a few minutes, then place pine nuts on each piece and press gently into the dough. Let rest for another 4 to 6 minutes, then bake 14 to 16 minutes, or until golden brown.

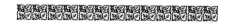

CHAPTER 10

Beverages
Bevande

ITALIAN COFFEE
Caffè Espresso

A double espresso! That's what I order after an Italian meal at one of my favorite haunts. The restaurant makes it in a large steam-producing machine that forces very hot water through the coffee to produce a deep, rich brew and serves it in a demitasse cup.

In some regions of Italy, espresso is served with a lemon peel. It is also often enhanced by the addition of liqueurs like anisette or sambuca. Milk is not added except in the morning, when it is scalded with a touch of cinnamon to make cappuccino. *A popular drink in the United States, caffè* latte *is usually half coffee and half milk.*

The popularity of espresso today is evident in the coffeehouses that have sprung up in both urban and resort areas, as well as in the sophisticated brewing machines people are using in their own homes.

Italian coffee beans are deep-roasted, very black, and ground to a very fine powder. You can buy Italian ground coffee in your supermarket for making espresso or drip coffee in one of the stove-top coffeemakers.

CHOCOLATE COFFEE AMARETTO

Cioccolata al Caffé e Amaretto

Here's a drink I invented years ago for some television and radio show appearances in the Great Northwest during blizzard months.

2 tablespoons brown sugar
½ cup amaretto liqueur
5 tablespoons espresso roast coffee
4 teaspoons unsweetened cocoa
4 cups water
Fresh lightly whipped cream

Serves 4

Mix the sugar and amaretto in the empty carafe of an automatic drip coffee maker, then brew the coffee in the usual way using the 5 tablespoons of espresso, 4 teaspoons of cocoa, and 4 cups of water.

Fill 4 glass coffee mugs and float a little whipped cream on top of each. Enjoy.

BELLINI

Harry's Bar in Venice features this drink that has reached our shores. I had the original at Harry's, then came home and created this recipe.

2 ounces peach juice (from fresh peaches or bottled concentrate)
4 ounces ice-cold champagne, sparkling wine, or dry white wine
Dash grenadine syrup (optional)

Serves 1

Combine all the ingredients and serve straight up.

SOME THINGS ITALIAN

Amaretto Liqueur. An almond-flavored liqueur.

Balsamic Vinegar (*Aceto Balsamico*). A slightly acidic, somewhat sweet vinegar made from pressed grapes aged in wood. It has a distinctive dark-amber color.

Basil. An aromatic herb, available fresh or dried, that has a sweet but strong taste. A main flavor contender in an Italian kitchen.

Bread Crumbs. Store-bought bread crumbs are sold flavored or plain, but crumbs can easily be made at home with hardened Italian bread.

Caciocavallo. A table and grating cheese that is mild when young and sharp as it becomes older. It is also available studded with whole peppercorns, making it a pungent companion for cured meats and assorted *antipasti*.

Cannellini. White kidney beans, sold both dried and canned.

Chicken Cutlets. White meat flattened for quick sautéing.

Crushed Red Pepper Flakes. Dried chile peppers crushed into flakes. In addition to their use in recipes, red pepper flakes make a table condiment that gives zing to sauces, vegetables, and soups.

Fennel Seeds. An anise-flavored spice similar to the fresh vegetable fennel. A little goes a long way.

Garlic Bulb/Clove. A whole head or bulb of garlic is composed of several individual cloves, which break away easily for recipe use.

Italian Parsley. Characterized by flat leaves in comparison to its curly counterpart, this parsley's less–acidic taste is best suited for Italian recipes.

Italian Sausage. Traditionally, a pork sausage, available in sweet or hot varieties, made with distinctive spices, especially fennel seeds (which give it an anise flavor).

Marsala. A dessert wine from Sicily with the rich, distinctive taste of burned sugar. Available dry (which is sweet) and sweet (which is sweeter).

Mascarpone. A sweet, creamy cheese slightly heavier than whipped cream.

Olive Oil. Italian olive oils are the pure products of the olive tree and have been filtered to remove sediment. For the past 8,000 years man has probably been enjoying this amazing tree and its fruits.

> **Extra Light.** Very mild-tasting and light in color; great for frying and ideal for baking.
>
> **Extra Virgin.** Made from the first cold pressing of the olives, with less than 1 percent acidity. Very fragrant, full-bodied, and greener in color than most other olive oils. Use it where oil is prominent, as in salads, dips, and sauces.
>
> **Pure.** A refined blend of olive oils having a less fruity taste. Use whenever the recipe calls for oil in general cooking.
>
> **Virgin.** Still from the first pressing but most probably heat is involved to create the pressure. This oil has a higher acidity. It is a fragrant addition to recipes using fish and in marinades.

Pancetta. A cured ham used similarly to bacon.

Parmesan (*Parmigiano*). A very hard cheese made with cow's milk, mild in flavor. It is used principally for grating but is also great for nibbling. Usually imported from Italy, Parmesan is also made domestically.

Pine Nuts (*Pignoli*). Really from pine trees! They look like tiny white beans and have a sweet taste.

Polenta. Cornmeal.

Prosciutto. A salted, air-cured ham, usually sliced very thin and eaten raw or sautéed as an ingredient in a recipe. The Italian variety is preferred, although prosciutto is also produced in the United States.

Ricotta. A cheese that is as creamy as cottage cheese and is made mainly from cow's milk. It is also available in low-fat and even no-fat varieties.

Romano. A hard grating cheese made with sheep's milk. It is sharper in favor than Parmesan. Although much is imported from Italy, Romano is also manufactured domestically.

Tomatoes, Canned Plum. Marzano, Italy, is known for its plum tomatoes, many of which are canned and exported. Of course, California is also a major packer. Usually plum tomatoes are canned with juice. Some are canned in a heavier purée. Experiment with brands of your choosing.

    Canned Whole and Peeled. Uncooked whole tomatoes are packed in tomato purée or tomato juice.

    Crushed. Whole, peeled, uncooked tomatoes that are crushed.

Tomato Paste. Made from tomatoes that were cooked for several hours, strained, and reduced to a thick concentrate.

Tomato Purée. Tomatoes are cooked briefly and strained to make a purée with a fairly thick consistency.

Tomato Sauce. Cooked tomatoes with the addition of seasonings and sometimes tomato paste.

THINGS TO KNOW

EQUIVALENTS

3 teaspoons	1 tablespoon
2 tablespoons	1 ounce
4 tablespoons	¼ cup
16 tablespoons	1 cup
2 cups	1 pint
4 cups	1 quart
1 pound granulated sugar	2 cups
1 pound confectioners' sugar	2⅓ cups
¼ pound butter or 1 stick	½ cup
1 pound all-purpose flour	4 cups sifted

INDEX